THE GENERATION
▪ OF IDEAS FOR ▪
NEW PRODUCTS

TREVOR SOWREY

PhD., MA (Cantab).,
Dip M, F Inst M., MCAM.

KOGAN
PAGE

I dedicate this book to my mother, the late Mrs Mary Sowrey.

First published in hardback in Great Britain by
Kogan Page Limited 1987
120 Pentonville Road, London N1 9JN

Reprinted with revisions in paperback in 1988

Copyright © Trevor Sowrey 1987

British Library Cataloguing in Publication Data

Sowrey, Trevor
  The generation of ideas for new
  products.
  1. New products
  I. Title
  658.5'75   HD69.N4

  ISBN 1-85091-433-8
  ISBN 1-85091-732-9 Pbk

Printed and bound in Great Britain

Contents

Preface

All too often an idea for a new product may be greeted with euphoria by management simply because ideas tend to be scarce within the company. If the idea then fails at a later stage in the development process, it often follows that disenchantment within the company may adversely affect the likelihood of future product development programmes. On some occasions even the career future of those directly involved may be affected.

Since the day I began the research work for this book, it has been my objective to help those managers in commerce and industry who are responsible for development to avoid the threat of this fate, by contributing material that can be used in practice to help them generate ideas that have the potential to become successful new products. The research is now completed; I hope that the publication of this book will enable my findings and conclusions to reach a wide audience of managers, and my objective be realized. Indeed, interviews that I have had with marketing managers as part of the research indicate that for them the book will be an essential reference, as it fills a gap in new product literature – the all-important area of idea generation.

Similarly, there is no book that deals adequately with idea generation for students on university postgraduate courses and those courses at polytechnics which, due to the initiative of the Council for National Academic Awards, now embrace the subject of innovation. Just as in industry itself, due to government pressure, there has come a slow and gradual appreciation of the need for innovatory policies, so those responsible for course design in higher education have come to appreciate that it is essential to prepare future managers so that they can meet this need.

To satisfy the requirements of both managers and students, the opening chapter outlines the central problem with regard to idea generation. In subsequent chapters, creativity, organizational structures, planning and the new product development programme are examined. In Chapter 6 over 60 techniques are described that can be used in the search for new product ideas. In this connection it would take a marketing manager many months of patient research through the existing literature to gather together a reasonable range that he could use. The next chapter reviews the available research studies in the UK dealing with idea generation, in order to indicate which techniques could be the most useful in practice. The unique nature of the book is that it is the first comprehensively to cover so many techniques in detail and give guidance based on research studies. In Chapter 8, the basic principles to follow are outlined as guidance. The last chapter illustrates the main theory of the book through the presentation of case studies. Finally, the Appendices list much of the important literature dealing with innovation so that the reader may follow up and delve deeper, if he so desires, into any aspect of new product development.

In the writing of this book I have drawn extensively on my own business experience and research, but this alone is never enough. A debt is owed to a considerable number of other writers. Acknowledgement to this work is made by the various chapter references and the Bibliography.

Trevor Sowrey
April 1987

Chapter 1
Idea Generation – the Neglected Stage in the Development Process

Since innovation is so important and since, as the Booz, Allen and Hamilton study[1] points out, three-quarters of development expense goes on unsuccessful products, it becomes vital to try and reduce this enormous wastage. To improve the strike rate of success to failure would be a significant step for any management.

(Randall G, 1980)[2]

INTRODUCTION

The conclusion of the author from his own practical experience is that generating ideas for new products is the most neglected stage in the development process. This was first appreciated when employed as a product manager with a leading international company some 20 years ago. The turnover of the company in the UK food market was then in excess of £80 million and the term 'marketing-oriented' could have been applied with justice to the company's operations. But it possessed only a very small new product department within its marketing organization. This consisted of a manager and two assistants with responsibility for the development of products new to the company. The development of line extensions was the responsibility of the product groups who controlled the existing brands. Once the new product department had developed a product it was handed over to one of the six product groups for test marketing.

With so few staff in the new product department it is not surprising that little attention could be paid to the time-consuming process of idea generation. Moreover, the staff involved tended to have been employed in this area more for their analytical skills than for their ability to think creatively. Top management, recognizing the importance of new products, had established a development department but had staffed it with people who reflected their own analytical business attitudes. Once established, the department received little encouragement. It was left alone and only appeared to be taken cognizance of when it was felt that cold analytical water needed to be poured on any creative idea which just by chance happened to arise.

Soon after, as new products manager with another company in the food industry, the author had the opportunity to see how far he personally could cope with the problem of generating ideas for new products. The company possessed a traditionally sales-oriented approach to its markets and the management had realized that there was a danger of being left behind by competitors unless the company became more marketing-oriented. As a result, a small marketing department was established and a new products manager appointed for the first time. It proved necessary to start from the very beginning and devise a corporate plan which included development objectives. With the establishment of a research and development (R and D) unit at the factory, attention had then to be paid to the task of generating suitable ideas for this unit to develop and to establish a system that would ensure that there was a continuous supply of good ideas available.

A system was established but without the help of the marketing literature of the day. Idea generation was a topic that was very much neglected both by the marketing academics and the professional marketers who had written on the subject of new products. Without the help of articles and books, every method that was instituted in the idea generation system had to be thought out from the beginning.

The above events occurred during the late 1960s. Certainly more has been written on new products since then. It is perhaps correct to say that every aspect of new product development has by now been adequately covered in marketing literature. Every aspect, that is, except one. Idea generation still remains a neglected topic. Yet this stage in the development process is one, if not the, most important as without ideas to develop, the other stages simply cannot take place. Ideas are needed to screen and analyse, and to develop into products which can first be product tested and then put into market test. Someone who is appointed today to the post of new products manager cannot rely on published marketing literature to help in building a system for generating ideas; it would require many months of patient research to sift through books and publications in order to gather together a comprehensive range of methods and techniques which could be used for this purpose.

THE PROBLEM

To the author this approach appears to be less than efficient. The likelihood is that if a good system for generating ideas cannot easily be established then it will not be established. The tendency will be for emphasis to be laid on the screening and testing of *ad hoc* ideas, as indicated by Parker (1982),[3] and not enough thought will be given to organizing procedures to ensure that new ideas of quality are available for screening and testing.

But, 'the effectiveness of subsequent stages in the process of developing promising new products is limited by the product ideas which were discovered.'[4] Unless the search process is so organized that it brings to management's attention those products which are likely to return satisfactory profits, a new product programme cannot function effectively. 'Firms which leave the process to hit or miss will, most of the time, do just that – miss.'[5]

The probable result will be that low quality ideas will go through the development process and 'frequently companies rush into design exercises without any clear specification for their new products'.[6] Product ideas which will not be successful in the market place will begin the costly, time-consuming process of being developed into tangible products. Some will be market tested and perhaps even launched on the market, for once a new product, however good or bad, gets a hold within a company it tends to gather momentum. Once it has got past a certain stage it often reaches a point where it appears almost impossible for management to decide not to put it on the market.

The inevitable result of such a situation must be that company management loses confidence in development which leads it to neglect the area entirely. Alternatively, many companies through fear of losing out in their markets may enter phases of 'development hysteria' from time to time. As a result rash decisions are made to go ahead on projects which would never have been considered if better ideas had been forthcoming.

Even where an idea generation system is established, such is the corporate inertia which can develop in some companies that there is a tendency for many to rely on methods and techniques which are considered 'safe'. Safe because they are easily understood as they produce ideas in a logical, straightforward manner.

Company managers are primarily employed to analyse data and make decisions based on their analysis. They are conditioned to a logical, matter-of-fact approach towards business. This is as it should be, but one regrettable consequence is that it may make many of them ill-equipped to handle decisions on anything arising in an apparently 'irrational' creative way. Many managers may be suspicious of anything which is new, particularly if it results from the creative, intangible aspects of life. As there is a natural human tendency also to prefer the security of the status quo, which might appear to be threatened by a new idea, then it is not surprising that creative techniques for generating ideas are perhaps avoided.

Instead, emphasis is laid on the collection of data and its analysis to yield new product ideas. This collective process embraces all forms of market studies and most standard market research methods, as they are numerate and logical in character. These analytical methods of course have value but perhaps receive too much attention at the expense of methods which rely on the creativity existing within an individual or group of people.

Thus it appears essential to establish within a company an effective idea generation system that embraces those techniques, both analytical and creative, that are likely to be the most productive in generating ideas for successful new products.

In order to be effective such a system should be continuous and systematic. To be continuous, the system would benefit from proper organizational control and to be systematic there is a need for the provision of adequate information by means of efficient planning procedures. Both an appropriate organization and correct planning will help to provide an encouraging environment that enables the system to be more fruitful creatively.

However, it should be acknowledged that within this generalized framework there is no single policy that can be universally applied. As outlined in Chapter 8, a policy should be followed situationally, wherein the complexity and variety of different environments and organizations are recognized. Each individual company can modify the common approach to that of the contingency or the situational approach, the approach which is applicable to its own situation and which will serve as its own individual framework for development.

THE PURPOSE OF THE BOOK

Given the problem described above, the purpose of this book is to provide those responsible for new product development within companies with a practical framework that will enable them to establish an effective system for generating ideas for new products. As a result of the adoption of such a framework, the whole development programme of the company should be able to function more efficiently and the rate of success to failure for new products be considerably improved.

To enable this framework to be established the author deals with the following areas:

1. A consideration of the creative process to identify the implications for idea generation systems.
2. A discussion concerning the various organizational structures and planning policies that may be adopted by companies in carrying out

their development activities and a review of the principles on which they are based, particularly the need to foster creativity.
3. A description of over 60 methods and techniques that can be used in the search for ideas for new products.
4. A review of available research studies dealing with idea generation within companies in order to help indicate which techniques may be the most successful in practice.
5. Conclusions as to the basic principles to follow as guidance to companies in the establishment of an idea generation system.
6. A presentation of three case studies to illustrate how the theory outlined in the book has been applied in real-life situations.
7. Finally, a listing of much of the published literature dealing with development so that company managers may follow up and delve deeper into any aspect of new product development.

The author's own business experience is mainly in consumer markets and these markets tend to demand the availability of a wide range of techniques to generate ideas. Therefore, there is a natural bias in the text towards consumer markets. But the areas outlined above and the conclusions drawn in the following chapters are also applicable to industrial goods markets.

DEFINITIONS

Before proceeding it would be advisable to define a number of terms; first of all the term 'new products', as different authors have diverse ideas as to what exactly new products can embrace. Confusion may arise from the fact that a product can be seen as 'new' from two points of view – that of the consumer and that of the company. In this book the author uses the term from the company's viewpoint as, after all, the book has been primarily written for the use of company management. As a result, new products are referred to in the sense of new brands or variations of existing brands, that is products which become a separate product item and have to be absorbed into the product mix. In the majority of cases the marketing of the brand will have entailed the creation of a separate marketing budget or even its own separate profit and loss account but it is not essential that this should have taken place. Thus the term covers two categories of new product:

1. New inventions: – embracing products new to both the company and the consumer.
2. Product modifications/differentiations: – embracing products new only to the company.

It is also necessary to clarify what is meant by success or failure, particularly when referred to in Chapter 7. In the 1960s and early 1970s, for many companies in the grocery market such as Cadbury-Schweppes and Nestlé, the idea became established that to be successful a new product should be capable of achieving around £1 million turnover on a national basis, although rapid inflation over recent years has of course weakened the acceptability of this criterion. The concept grew perhaps in response to the feeling that some sort of criterion should be set; possibly it was seldom used as a sales target, as even today for a few companies the £1 million target can often be hard to achieve.

In 1979, H Lavery, managing director of Cadbury-Typhoo[7] believed that a new product in the food market would require a sales level of £4 million to be regarded as successful. In practice, however, many companies do not appear to set definite targets and tend to judge each product on its own individual merits. Part of the reason for this is probably the non-linear relationship between profit and turnover, for many low-volume products in fact can be profitable. But subjective reasons can also often be advanced as to why a product is successful: after so much time and effort in bringing about a new product launch many companies are loth to admit failure even if the justification for continuing the product is flimsy. For example, Crosse and Blackwell (a division of Nestlé) continued for some years to sell Maggi packet soups as a grocery store brand in spite of its inability to make an impression on the market against competition from Knorr and Batchelors.

Some of the reasons for considering a product successful, even where the profit contribution is not substantial, are real enough. Utilizing excess plant capacity and the resulting effect on factory overheads, long-term growth potential, the enhancement of company image, filling in a product line, can be valid enough reasons by themselves for influencing management's judgement on success or failure. But there is a danger that such reasons may be put forward in hope rather than in fact. It should be simple for a company to judge if a product is successful by asking if after launch the results meet the company's development criteria; but judgement is difficult if such criteria do not exist or if, where they do exist, they are not always adhered to.

Valid judgement can also be difficult because one man's success can be another man's failure; what is acceptable to one company might not be acceptable to another. A successful new product for 'Smiths Soap Company' might have been rejected at an early stage in development by Procter and Gamble or Lever Brothers.

Because of the problem of establishing general criteria applicable to all companies there is no alternative but to define success and failure in terms of the individual company. A successful product is defined as one considered by the company marketing it to be a success. It has passed through the development process and been launched into the market, achieving a level of sale and profit satisfactory to the company. Conversely, a product is judged to be a failure if the company deems it to be so. It has been rejected at some stage in the development process or judged to be a failure in test market or withdrawn soon after launch.

It is acknowledged that subjective factors may influence the company in its decision as to success or failure. These factors may be valid but it is easy enough in practice to stretch such reasoning to cover unreasonable situations. However, it is felt that there is no satisfactory alternative than to rely on the company's judgement on its own products.

It should be stated also that no attempt has been made to grade success into various levels such as very, moderately or slightly successful. For the reasons mentioned above it is felt that such an exercise would be impractical.

Finally, it should be stated that in relation to idea generation the terms 'sources', 'techniques' and 'methods' are sometimes used in this book as though they are interchangeable. It is acknowledged that on the evidence of any dictionary the terms do differ. Also some product ideas can be clearly identified as coming from a definite source of origin (such as the R and D department) and others can be attributed to a definite technique (such as gap analysis). But with many ideas it could bring confusion in the text to attempt to distinguish between the terms. For example, a research survey of trade opinion might be regarded as a source, a technique or a method.

Therefore, where applicable the term 'source' is used to denote a point of origin and the terms 'techniques' and 'methods' are used to denote forms of procedure, but in order to add to the clarity of the text the terms are also used on occasions as though they are interchangeable in meaning.

REFERENCES

1 Booz, Allen and Hamilton Inc, *The Management of New Products*, 1966.
2 Randall G, *Managing New Products*, British Institute of Management, 1980.
3 Parker R C, *The Management of Innovation*, J Wiley, 1982.
4 Pessemier E A, *New Product Decisions – An Analytical Approach*, McGraw Hill, 1966.
5 Buggie F D, 'How to innovate', *Management Today*, September 1981.
6 Oakley M, *Managing Product Design*, Weidenfeld and Nicolson, 1984.
7 Bacot E (ed), *Marketfact*, No 48, 22 March 1979.

Chapter 2 Creativity in Development

THE PROBLEM

The one ingredient that is vital in new product development, but at the same time defies adequate understanding, is creativity. It is an intangible that never shows up in the marketing plan and yet it can be the single factor which most often determines success or failure. The development of a new product is not usually the result of a process which is completely rational in nature. It is similar to scientific research where the investigator starts from existing knowledge and proceeds by a mixture of reason and imagination. But the final creative leap is not entirely under our control; it comes as a burst of inspiration, moving from the way things are to something new by synthesizing previously unconnected matrices of thought. It is this process which Koestler (1964)[1] termed 'bisociative' thinking, a word he coined to distinguish the creative act from the routines of associative thinking.

'Although millions of words have been written about creativity a commonly recognized, all-purpose definition is lacking.'[2] As a result, 'there are almost as many ways of defining creativity as there are writers on the subject'.[3] The capacity to be creative is not subject to theoretical analysis as the elements operate largely at a subconscious level and cannot be communicated easily to others. Researchers cannot enter the minds of individuals to study what occurs. The very breadth of the creative process, embracing such apparent contradictions as artistic creativity and scientific research, presents a difficulty. 'Like the toddler chasing her butterfly I was sure I would catch it (the creative process) while pursuing it. But now that I have arrived at the end, I see that it has got away again.'[4]

A THEORY

A theory as to what happens in the process of creative thinking would be beneficial, providing a coherent framework within which useful generalizations could be made and in turn verified by applying them to specific problems. To this end Gordon (1956)[5] conducted experiments in group creativity. His objective was to devise a theory that would make conscious and performable at will a process that is usually left to inspiration. He identified in his study six phases that occurred whenever creativity was at work. The first was the recognition that every creative synthesis has its beginning in the commonplace. The second was the continual shifting back and forth between involvement and detachment. The third was the capacity to speculate, leading to the fourth which was the deferment of immediate gains in favour of more rewarding future gains. The fifth was the realization that in the process of creation the object being worked upon appears to take on an independent life of its own, so that in the last phase it develops a purpose and appears to take a hand in fashioning itself.

Nyström (1979)[3] also devised a theoretical background in a model which summarized some earlier research. He divided the creative process into four stages. In the first stage of preparation, a large amount of material is collected from many sources. The emphasis at this stage is on a wider, intuitive type of thinking in which lateral thinking, exploring many possibilities, rather than vertical thinking, concentrating on a single line of reasoning, is of great value. This is followed by an incubation stage when conscious concentration on the problem ends and subconscious data processing may be assumed to take place. If the subconscious thought process is successful the next stage of insight takes place, that is a discovery, usually sudden, of previously unrelated ideas conceived as a solution to the problem. This leads to the final stage of verification, which is concerned with formal analysis of the results against objective criteria.

THE CREATIVE INDIVIDUAL

The difficulties involved in analysing the creative process have meant that much of the research has been concerned with two areas. First, the attributes and personality of a creative individual and second, the aspects of the environment that foster creativity. A great deal of literature now exists on the attributes of the creator and Barron (1969)[6] has described a large amount of the research work. However, the findings must remain debatable as little progress has been made in achieving acceptable objective criteria which would enable a creative person to be easily identified. Some investigators assume that their subjects are creative on reputation where qualified 'experts' have identified creators in a current environment situation, or the general consensus of historical opinion has been made the arbiter.

Although debatable, the findings suggest that in general the personality behind creative thinking must possess three broad attributes. First of all he must possess knowledge as a basic requirement, as nothing can be made from nothing. Knowledge acts as a store of blocks to allow the building of new combinations. This aspect is perhaps best illustrated in the research findings of Newell, Shaw and Simon (1962),[7] which show that the typical features of creative thinking, at least in mathematics and chess playing, are amenable to computer simulation. Andrus (1968)[8] sees the computer playing an important role in creativity in business. He distinguishes two kinds of creativity, one largely the result of hard work in sorting and combining elements of existing knowledge. For this the computer can be used, freeing management for the second more mystical type of creativity. But as Andrus states, the computer's ability to solve problems creatively is limited according to its program. The computer can only be creative within previously stated knowledge as programmed guidelines.

Whether these systematic creative acts are worthy of the term 'creative' is questionable. To Osborn (1953)[9] an individual's mental capacities comprise four functions: absorptive (observe and apply attention); retentive (memorize and recall); reasoning (analyse and judge); creative (visualize and generate ideas). Although computers can perform the first three functions, they cannot perform the fourth. Certainly, the possession of knowledge alone does not make an individual creative. Most people fail to use much of their useful knowledge in solving a problem even though they may have access to analogies relevant to the problem in hand.

Osborn's first three functions relate to the second basic requirement for creative thinking, that is the possession of intellectual abilities, for they enable knowledge to be used effectively. The research findings of MacKinnon (1962)[10] suggest that a reasonably high level of intellect is required for creativity, but beyond that point being more or less intelligent is not determinative of the level of creativeness. However, the addition of mental skills to knowledge does not necessarily make an individual creative.

The factors which determine an individual's creativeness appear to be personal rather than intellectual. In reviewing a variety of research, Shapiro (1968)[11] believes that there is a good deal of evidence to suggest that creative individuals differ significantly from non-creative individuals in certain personality traits, and it is these emotional aspects of personality appertaining to attitude and mood, which make a person more likely to use his knowledge and intelligence to develop new ideas.

These aspects of personality, around which romantic speculation has built up, have developed in the individual from a combination of inheritance and childhood experience and as a result are difficult to identify. But research has indicated that perhaps creative individuals possess certain attributes in common. One of these characteristics is a perceptive attitude towards life (MacKinnon, 1962)[10] which results in the individual living a life that is more spontaneous rather than controlled and orderly. The creative individual is more open to the richness and complexity of experience as a result. He is also a non-conformist by nature (Cattell and Butcher, 1968),[12] with a high degree of intellectual self-sufficiency, accepting nothing on faith just because it has the voice of authority behind it (MacKinnon, 1962).[10] He believes in self-regulation for himself rather than in externally imposed control (Cattell and Butcher, 1968).[12] Although he rejects regulation by others, he requires from his immediate environment a degree of psychological safety where he feels that his worth is recognized and where he has the freedom to express his ideas without strong external evaluation (Rogers, 1954).[13] He requires not only freedom of expression but an environment where he is understood empathically so that he can fulfil his need to communicate about his creation (Rogers, 1954).[13]

These traits do not embrace all the personality factors that have been identified but they are characteristics which are significant and which can be accommodated within, and affected by, the business environment in order to encourage creative thinking within an organization.

THE ORGANIZATIONAL ENVIRONMENT

Tests conducted in the sphere of education to evaluate the effect of formal and informal schools on creativity (Haddon and Lytton, 1968)[14] produced evidence that informality provides an environment which results in a high level of creative thinking ability. It would appear reasonable to assume that an informal atmosphere, be it at the level of a school organization or a business organization, could provide an environment where the personality traits of a creative person would be likely to be most satisfactorily accommodated.

Although it is not easy to translate this informality into the ideal factors that should be present within a business, there are several attributes which can be built into the organizational framework. These will be dealt with more fully in Chapter 3 but mention can be made of the more significant points. A flat management hierarchy with an informal, loose working structure is of value, as a creative person benefits from encouraging interaction with his colleagues. An organization which does not immerse its creative people in routine administrative activity is also important. If employees are not allowed time to question and do not possess the freedom to roam free mentally then it is unlikely that creative ideas will be produced. 'Passive acceptance of too much control is not the hallmark of the true innovator.'[15] High quality leadership also has a place, as performance is improved when people feel part of a group that is headed by a competent and respected chief who acts as a democratic and consensus-seeking leader. The support of top management is also important to help overcome the opposition that new ideas face if they are seen as a threat to the status quo.

Knowledge, too, can be built into a company's *modus operandi*. A corporate plan which includes definitive development objectives based on market and consumer research provides the bricks the creative mind requires to build new combinations. The setting of these objectives gives a direction to creative thinking so that the minimum of time is wasted on the exploration of opportunities which the company is not in a position to take advantage. (Planning for development is covered in greater detail in Chapter 4.)

Beyond the environment of the company itself there are wider factors which mould the situation in which the creative individual finds himself. These are outside the control of the company but nevertheless they act as a stimulant or otherwise to creativity. The actions of government through the manipulation of financial measures such as investment grants and taxation can create a climate which encourages creativity. As Brozen (1951)[16] points out, where capital is restricted the rate of invention and innovation slows down, to be replaced by the lower risk policy of imitation. The educational system in a country will also affect creativity; on the evidence of Parnes (1963),[17] an individual's creative ability is frequently repressed by his education.

CONCLUSION

The last point is of some significance: the effect on creativity of the wider environment is beyond the control of a company, but there can be implications which have a bearing on organizational practices within companies. Osborn (1953)[9] quotes a good deal of evidence to support the view that all human beings possess, to a greater or lesser degree, creative imagination. As stated by Rickards (1985),[18] 'creativity has been misunderstood by managers if they have equated it with a rare talent . . . This is the élitist view.' But the very circumstances of living and a conformist educational system encourage the exercise of the judicial side of the mind and the neglect of the creative. As a result inhibitions develop which tend to rigidize our thinking. Some of the creative techniques outlined in Chapter 6 can help individuals to overcome these inhibitions.

Companies recognizing that all employees have creative potential – that creation is not reserved for just a few people, usually of senior management status – can perhaps obtain substantial gains. 'Genius is rare and thinly spread and few companies can be expected to employ outstanding entrepreneurs.'[19] Therefore they must be prepared to encourage and have faith in creative techniques which involve a wide variety of people. The need for ideas is dealt with in Chapter 5, but the need is such that company management should not neglect creative methods because they appear informal and do not directly involve the company's 'experts'. This is the very nature of the creative process which does not conform to established procedures. It can be more productive to keep all sources open and to place some emphasis on those techniques which involve a wide variety of people. In this way the total flow of ideas can be strengthened and the chances of a successful new product arising from the development programme considerably increased.

Several research studies which are concerned with sources and techniques are examined in Chapter 7, but it should be mentioned here that the findings of the fourth study not only endorse the value of creative techniques but also indicate that the more techniques used that involve a wide variety of people, the more successful products a company is likely to be able to launch. At the time of the study, companies such as Findus and Reckitts Household Division, for example, who were utilizing a wide variety of techniques also had a good track record for successful new products.

REFERENCES

1 Koestler A, *The Act of Creation*, Hutchinson, 1964.
2 Holt K, *Product Innovation Management*, Butterworths, 1983.
3 Nyström H, *Creativity and Innovation*, John Wiley and Sons, 1979.
4 Rokeach M, 'In pursuit of the creative process', *The Creative Organization* (ed Steiner G A), University of Chicago Press, 1965.
5 Gordon W J J, 'An operational approach to creativity', *Harvard Business Review*, Nov-Dec 1956.
6 Barron F, *Creative Persons and Creative Process*, Holt, Rinehart and Winston, 1969.
7 Newell A, Shaw T C and Simon H A, 'The process of creative thinking', *Contemporary Approaches to Creative Thinking* (ed Gruber H E), Atherton Press, 1962.
8 Andrus R R, 'Creativity: a function for computers or executives', *Journal of Marketing*, Vol 32, April 1968.
9 Osborn A F, *Applied Imagination*, Charles Scribners' Sons, 1953.
10 MacKinnon D W, 'The personality correlates of creativity' (1962), *Creativity* (ed Vernon P E), Penguin Books, 1970.
11 Shapiro R J, 'The criterion problem' (1968), *Creativity* (ed Vernon P E), Penguin Books, 1970.
12 Cattell R B and Butcher H J, 'Creativity and personality' (1968), *Creativity* (ed Vernon P E), Penguin Books, 1970.
13 Rogers C R, 'Towards a theory of creativity' (1954), *Creativity* (ed Vernon P E), Penguin Books, 1970.
14 Haddon F A and Lytton H, 'Teaching approach and divergent thinking abilities' (1968), *Creativity* (ed Vernon P E), Penguin Books, 1970.
15 Whitfield P R, *Creativity in Industry*, Penguin Books, 1975.
16 Brozen Y, 'Invention, innovation and imitation', *American Economic Review*, Vol 41, Part 1, 1951.

17 Parnes S J, 'Education and creativity', *Teachers College Record*, Vol 64, 1963.
18 Rickards T, *Stimulating Innovation*, Frances Pinter, 1985.
19 Parker R C, *Guidelines for Product Innovation*, British Institute of Management, 1980.

Chapter 3 Organizing for Development

THE PROBLEM

'If the community sets out to encourage innovation it is by no means clear how best it could be brought about, what institutional framework will most effectively stimulate and encourage the man with the powers of originality, most swiftly distinguish between the channels open to progress and the blind alleys and most thoroughly glean the economic harvest from innovation.'[1] This sentiment, expressed with regard to types of insitution, appears to be equally valid for the types of organizational framework that can be adopted by an institution. The major problems that a company encounters in new product development appear to be those that are concerned with organization. Eight out of every 10 companies in one major study of development[2] mentioned organization as a difficult area and over half the problems mentioned were concerned with this area, a rate which was four-and-a-half times greater than the next most frequently mentioned problem. These problems were specifically organizational, that is they arose from the way people work together, but most of the other problems reported – poor control, poorly defined objectives, inadequate business analysis, inadequate idea generation – also tend to arise as a result of organizational weaknesses.

THE NEED FOR ORGANIZATION

Without effective organization in a company there will not be effective innovation. A company has to make a conscious effort to plan for its future needs and allow these needs to be catered for by providing an organizational framework to look after innovation. The major objective of any company is to make profits and thus the short-term needs tend to rule. Even where longer-term planning takes place, there usually comes a period of stress in the life of any firm when the present is of prime concern and the future is allowed to look after itself. This preoccupation with the present has been reinforced in recent years with the increased emphasis placed on cost accounting, often resulting in a state of mind which regards creative research as a 'luxury'. This cost consciousness sharpens the traditional conflicts between the creative person and the administrators and as the latter often tend to rise highest in the hierarchical structure there are many who can crush creative ideas as they arise unless creativity, as a function, is protected in the company's organizational structure. New ideas may be opposed on the level of unconscious activity because they are not understood. They may also be opposed on the level of conscious conspiracy because new ideas mean change and are therefore a threat to the security of the status quo. However, it must be stated that some companies mainly multinationals, appear to have freed themselves from an inhibiting preoccupation with the present. For example, among the companies which have developed creativity training over the years are General Electric and PPG Industries in the USA and Unilever and IBM in Europe.

To encourage creative innovation a company needs an organizational framework that acknowledges responsibility for development. An effective organization is the basis of an effective development programme because it allows:

1. Forward planning based on company resources and the requirements of the market.
2. New ideas to arise and be recognized that meet the objectives of this plan.
3. Tasks to be identified and responsibility delegated.
4. Effective communication and a co-ordinated effort to get things done.

TYPES OF ORGANIZATION

Several basic forms of internal organization have been developed over time in an effort to meet these requirements.

The research and development department – top management

Historically innovation took place on the initiative of production (which had an R and D role) and occasionally on the initiative of top management. When a prototype new product was devised it was shown by production directly to top management for approval. This type of organization, shown in Figure 3.1(a), is still present in many companies. A variant on the pattern, where R and D forms a separate department to production, is also quite common (see Figure 3.1(b)). This latter form is often established when higher than average quality control standards are required and as a result it is felt that a department independent of production is necessary.

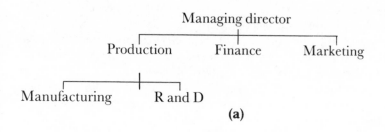

(a)

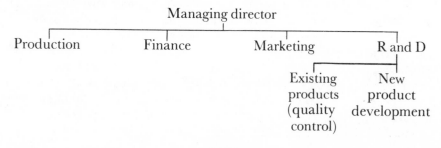

(b)
Figure 3.1

The advantage for development activities with both these forms is that communication is direct to the top and thus action can be swift. The major weakness is that ideas can rarely come from marketing-oriented planning and as a result, the products may not be directly related to consumer needs. Thus the company may waste a lot of time on developing products that no one wants. In both situations there is a natural tendency for too much time to be spent on quality control and too little on actual development work. Even where a separate development section is established within the R and D unit the working time of this section may be appropriated for existing products during busy periods.

Companies such as Schreiber Furniture, Hovis and Lockwoods Foods have all used the simple structures outlined above. The structures are most commonly found among companies marketing industrial or commodity-type consumer products. But the form of organization that any one company adopts, whatever its products, may be subject to change; indeed, these changes tend to be progressive as the company adapts to changes both in its market and in its industry.

The new products committee

The natural successor to top management's control of R and D is for authority to be vested in a new products committee (see Figure 3.2). Its members represent the principle functional areas of the business and they are often the heads of departments. This representative membership is the major weakness because human beings are usually captives of their own environment and thus the minimum of creativity will abound. At best the new products committee is only suitable for small-scale programmes. Its members can be assigned overall responsibility to act as a search team leading idea generation, to be responsible for evaluation and to act as a project team responsible for development. But if the rate of development increases, the committee can become unwieldy as action is difficult to carry out in a situation where the detailed workload becomes heavy. To overcome the problem the committee can appoint one or two full-time staff assistants to do the investigatory detail work and provide day-to-day continuity, as at Lyons Soft Drinks at one time. The obvious next step, as the workload increases, is for the staff assistants to be assigned to the marketing department which then assumes responsibility for development. The new products committee is often retained after this step to act as an overall policy making and review board. This latter step has taken place at many companies at one time or another, such as Findus, T I Croda and Reckitts Pharmaceuticals.

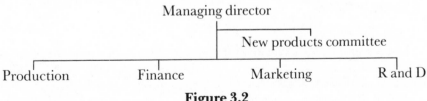

Figure 3.2

Product managers

Placing responsibility for development with the product management team in the marketing department is a popular way of handling new products in the UK. It has been used by Lever Brothers, Lyons Bakery, Whitbread, Fisons, Van den Berghs, Pedigree Petfoods and many other well-known companies. With this form of organization two basic types of structure can exist, as shown in Figure 3.3.

A product manager for a number of existing brands may in addition have responsibility for the development of new products in similar markets to his existing brands. Thus the same individual has responsibility for both existing products and new product development. On the other hand, responsibility may be functionally divided so that there are product managers handling existing brands and others handling product development. To prevent the organization becoming too diffuse from the point of view of control, the product managers often (though not necessarily) report to another individual (usually with the title marketing manager or group product manager) between themselves and board level.

The major limitation with both forms of organization is the inevitable danger that development activities will be neglected. Certainly, when one individual is responsible for both existing brands and development, not enough attention may be paid to the search for new products because of the demands in terms of both time and money from existing brands, which are the profit makers. In this respect it can well be argued that new product development is not a part-time job, part-time in the sense that current brands come first when both they and development activities are handled by one person. It is unlikely that the person concerned will have either the time or the motivation to look for a new product. He is employed primarily to manage an existing business and he is judged on this rather than on his new product performance. Dividing the brand group functionally into existing product and new product personnel attempts to get away from this dichotomy and remove the worst of its possible effects.

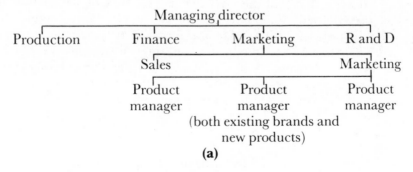

(a)

(b)

Figure 3.3

The new products department

It is but a short step in organizational terms from new product managers to a functionally based new products department. Like the product management system, many well-known companies have used this type of organization. These have included Cadbury-Typhoo, Findus, Johnson and Johnson, Quaker, United Biscuits and K P Foods. But there are variations in the structure, as shown in Figure 3.4, with responsibility in the majority being to the marketing director, in others to the managing director and in some to a new products or R and D director. The department may have line responsibility for new products until the end of test market or the product may be handed over to existing products marketing before test market. In some cases it may exist purely in an advisory staff function with emphasis perhaps on co-ordination as the major responsibility. But one common thread, whatever different form the structure may take, is that the department is separated from the day-to-day responsibilities of making a profit and can concentrate attention on development. In the Booz, Allen and Hamilton Study,[2] 86 per cent of companies in the USA at that time were reported as organizing their development work through a separate new products department. One possible drawback is that the department could become remote from the rest of the company and be looked on as 'a collection of impractical backroom egg-heads'.[3] To overcome this it is necessary to lay down procedures to ensure that good communication channels exist with other departments. To encourage integration further, representatives from the other major departments concerned with the development process can be assigned to work on a part-time basis within the new products department.

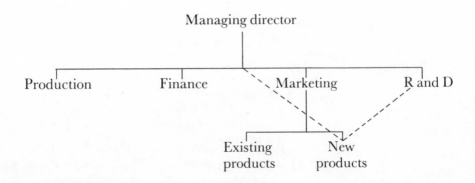

Figure 3.4

The diversification department

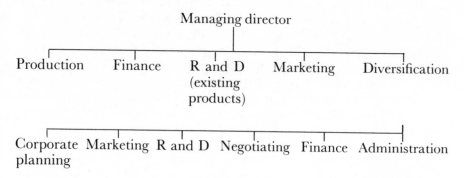

Figure 3.5

The logical extension to the new products department is the diversification department, which is structured as a department separate from the marketing department and existing as a parallel organization, as shown in Figure 3.5. The top executive of the department is a board director responsible to the managing director and equal in status to the marketing director. As a result, a complete separation occurs between the current operation and development. Reporting to the diversification director would be a small group of marketing people, accountants and R and D chemists/engineers. Also the corporate planning function could come within this sphere. In addition to its own marketing section the department would have its own R and D separate from the central R and D and a specialist negotiating section responsible for the purchase of co-packed products and for acquisition negotiations.

Structures vary because of the resource implication, but such an organization could be made to encompass the responsibilities illustrated in Figure 3.6. The advantage of this structure is that, as a result of being away from current problems, the whole area of future needs and requirements appears important to company employees as a whole. Moreover, the department can adopt a balanced attitude towards development, beginning with the establishment of corporate objectives and long-term plans and then proceeding to implement these plans, through the wide spectrum of new product development, market development and acquisitions. As a result the company can adopt a fully planned approach rather than dealing with future needs in an *ad hoc* and sporadic fashion.

As with a new products department, there is the danger that a diversification department could be looked on as an ivory tower, and this could result in a problem when handing over developed products and transferring knowledge concerning these products to the marketing department. There is no easy answer to this problem. Good communications with all other departments will help, but this is always a difficult objective to achieve. Certainly the major advantage overall is that a balanced attitude towards future company needs is more likely to be established and with good top management this realization can percolate the whole company, counteracting any ivory tower attitudes that may develop among employees. Few companies in the UK have ever adopted any form of diversification department, probably because of the resources required, but H J Heinz has been a notable exception.

As early as 1962 Theodore Levitt[3] suggested the need for a separate organization to deal with development as a whole. His 'blue skies planning committee' was responsible for monitoring the social environment on a continuous basis in order to spot possible business opportunities. It was to be staffed by people removed from day-to-day operating responsibilities, reporting directly to someone at policy level in order to avoid the conservative influences present in most companies that tend to produce conventionally both in people and ideas.

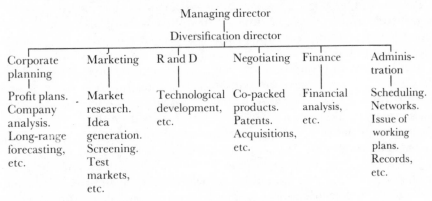

Figure 3.6

Venture management

A venture group, also known as a project team or a task force, consists of a team of individuals drawn from various departments working on a development project, some full time and others part time. Responsibility for guiding the team is in the hands of a venture or project manager who stays with the project from inception to commercialization. He acts as a general manager for the project, drawing in people from different departments as the need arises, some of whom will remain full time, while others will leave the team once their contribution has been made, perhaps to return to it at a later stage. The group is able to draw on the parent company for many of the service functions, for example purchasing, accounting, legal. Only when these services grow to the point where they occupy an individual full time on the project need he be transferred into the group.

The venture team concept is most applicable to large companies; it combines the advantages of the extensive technical and financial resources available in most large companies with the entrepreneurial spirit, single-mindedness and ease of communication found in a small business. The chief deterrent to the success of many new products is often the fact that the company concentrates on today's business and tends to resist change, whereas the venture team is specifically created to bring about change in a product area.

Venture management lays emphasis on the evaluation of projects and in a company where several venture teams are developing separate products, each project is viewed not in isolation but in relation to all the other projects, enabling go/no go decisions to be made on which to progress according to the resources available. For this reason criteria are essential to appraise the value of the venture and if at any time these indicators show that venture goals seem unattainable, reduction or termination of effort should be considered.

If the project is successful and the product reaches the market, the venture team can be disbanded and the product handed over to others. Alternatively, some or all of the team can become a permanent unit with operating responsibility for the product. The timing of this transition, whichever path is chosen, may be when the commercial plant comes into operation or, if problems arise, when reasonable market penetration is achieved.

Disadvantages arise if the team is disbanded and the product has to be handed over to the marketing department. As in the case of the diversification department, only a limited number of people will have been involved in the project and the necessary 'transfer of knowledge' could be difficult. There is also another possible weakness in that with several venture teams in existence a spirit of competition can arise. This is an advantage so far as obtaining action is concerned but it is too much to ask one person, the venture manager, both to fight for and promote his product on the one hand and to evaluate it objectively on the other. To some extent this can be overcome, if a new products committee is also established to review project progress.

Another limitation is that the venture team operates in a situation where the marketable product idea already exists. The responsibility is essentially one of commercializing new products, that is facilitating the introduction and increasing the probability of commercial success. But marketable ideas have to come from somewhere. It would be possible to start a venture team as, say, a group of two, a marketing person and a member of the R and D team, charged with the task of first generating an idea and then developing it, with other personnel being added to the group as circumstances dictate.

Alternatively, the task of idea generation (and overall planning) could be handled by a group of staff specialists, with new ideas for products being reviewed by the new products committee. In effect the whole task of development would then be handled by a three-pronged organization, as shown in Figure 3.7, with a committee reviewing not only overall development plans but also ideas generated from the staff team and proposals from venture managers, the latter becoming actively involved at the business analysis stage.

In this way some of the limitations of venture management can be overcome, but it is important not to stifle venture managers through too bureaucratic an organizational framework. For the system is essentially 'based on the "mission" approach requiring an acceptance that new product programmes should be viewed as ventures handled by a small team guiding the project from beginning to end'.[4] They should exist as separate entities within the company. Indeed, they can be treated as separate profit and loss centres each with its own budget, that is as small independent businesses within the company.

Defining the concept strictly there is a distinction between a venture team and a project group. The former is an extension of the latter in that it is completely outside the normal organizational structure and has its own funding. Pioneered by Du Pont in the 1960s, it was estimated[5] that 25 to 33 per cent of the largest US companies had such teams by the mid-1970s. Organizational problems and the effect of changes in the world economy on the business climate led to their decline. But despite its former popularity in the USA (for example, the Ford Mustang was developed by a venture team), it has never been popular in the UK. However, in both countries the basic concept appears to continue on a smaller scale as the project team or group and over half the UK companies in the study by Randall (1980)[5] used a project team from time to time.

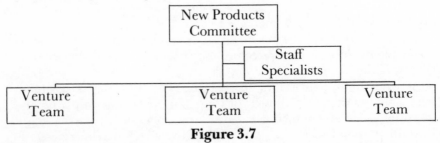

Figure 3.7

GENERAL PRINCIPLES OF ORGANIZATION

Establishing an organizational framework for development is not an end in itself. Top management cannot create the organization and then leave it to survive or fall, but must recognize that in order to encourage the most efficient development work it is necessary actively to adopt certain broad courses of action.

Involvement of top management

Top management should be fully committed and involved in the development process, taking an active not a passive role. New product consciousness is a company-wide policy. It involves everyone and is part of the corporate personality. Stimulating new product thinking is not a matter of just hiring a man; it must start at the very top and infiltrate the whole company. Company employees take their lead from above and if top management is actively interested in development then everyone else will be. In practice top management should ensure that it holds and is seen to hold the final decision with regard to setting objectives, recommending development projects and approving final commercialization. It should take an active interest in all projects, emphasizing long-term results and not just tolerating failures but expecting them within certain limits. Efforts should be made to facilitate communication, delegate responsibility and encourage informal working methods in the development area. The commitment adopted by the company as a whole to new products will be set by the management style emanating from above. Without an overall commitment from top management a weak organizational structure will result.

The top person

To reinforce this commitment it is important that someone senior heads up the development team. It is a bad mistake to staff this top position with a person of either inadequate prestige or inadequate background. One characteristic of successful innovating companies revealed by Project Sappho[6] was that such companies gave the responsibility for development to someone senior and gave him the necessary authority to do his job. The person appointed should be a competent and respected leader, preferably someone democratic by nature, that is, a consensus-seeking leader; someone who believes in a flat hierarchy without tiered levels of seniority but with informal co-ordination replacing autocratic direction.

All too often the top job is given to someone because it partly fits into his area of experience. But the person chosen for this job should also possess

33

some element of creativity, if only to increase the chances that some creative people will be employed in his department. He does not have to be that rare creative person who is capable of conceiving original ideas, but should possess some of the much commoner form of creativity and have the capacity to enlarge existing ideas. Creativity is difficult to identify; few companies will know which of their employees are capable of original thinking. Indeed some may fail to recognize the fundamental need for creativity in new product development. But if the top person is creative then it is more likely that he will be able to recognize this attribute in others.

Two kinds of people are needed in the conception and formulation of a new product – 'creators' to give birth to and shape the initial idea and 'administrators' who can mould the idea into practicality. All too often there is the situation of a development team consisting wholly of unadventurous 'administrators' working on second-rate ideas of their own.

The development team

The development process brings creators and administrators together and in so doing it involves all sides of the company's activities. Development requires a blend of marketing skills, R and D, production and finance as a basic minimum. Ideally, representatives from the major departments should be in the development team, working there as a full-time assignment. In this way the pulls, both real and emotional, of their own departments are left behind, which allows the team to achieve a more efficient co-ordinated effort. But it must be recognized that in many companies such an arrangement is just not economic.

Working relationships

Within the team itself relationships should be based on a loose working structure and hierarchical status structures avoided. In this connection it is the person at the top who will set the style for the team. Informality can encourage creativity and lead to better communication and co-ordination and thus to greater efficiency. Research in 1961[7] and again in 1985[8] has suggested that in highly technical industries and those in which change is rapid, loose working arrangements can be important in order to absorb the expected frequent changes of direction in development. In a mechanistic structure with a formal hierarchy of authority, communication and control may crack under the strain. A loose working, organic framework is more appropriate to changing conditions which give rise to fresh problems that cannot be broken down automatically into functional tasks. A network pattern, lateral communication, continuous redefinition of tasks through group interaction are more suitable in these circumstances. The working relationships resulting from an organic structure are essential for a development team. In addition the company as a whole is in a better position to adapt itself to change.

These factors are important in dynamic technical markets but are probably valid also for all companies, irrespective of the type of market in which they participate. The author has worked for a medium-sized company (500 employees) in the food and drinks industry which, in reorganizing itself from a sales to a marketing orientation, undertook a vigorous and successful development programme and in so doing the whole company unconsciously adopted organic procedures.

However, problems tend to arise in the situation where a company with a strong hierarchic structure tries to adapt itself to conditions of change. More personnel are usually employed in a new department to cope with this change and inevitably an organic pattern develops in the new department. A wise top management will accept this but often the result is that friction develops between the new department and top management, which is unhappy with working relationships it does not understand and so attempts are made to impose a hierarchic structure. Again, the author has worked for a large company (25,000 employees) in the consumer goods market with a strong hierarchic tradition, which was attempting both to become marketing-oriented and to establish a planned development programme. But internal pressures, resulting from the co-existence of an organic marketing department grafted on to an authoritarian mechanistic structure proved too great, resulting in a low level of marketing efficiency and a high marketing staff turnover.

The ability of a company to accept organic procedures during periods of change is probably related to the size of the company. The Burns and Stalker study[7] concerns only technical markets and only those, such as electronics, in which change is rapid. Such companies tend to be at an extreme, particularly as in the study the majority were small in size and consequently more able to adopt organic procedures in the company as a whole. But size is probably the major criterion for all markets. The bigger the company, the more likely it is that autocratic and hierarchic structures become embedded over time. The company tends to become sluggish by virtue of the delegation of authority and responsibility and the complication of the decision-making process which accompanies such delegation. It becomes unresponsive to change, strongly resisting new working relationships that may be adopted in the development team.

However, new product development is concerned with the change involved in producing good ideas and turning them into profitable products. The company may not be able to move easily from a hierarchical position, but the way the development team is structured often needs to be radically different from the rest of the company because creativity is not suited to traditional forms of control. So many of the activities of a company are administrative and routine in nature and subject to control mechanisms, to ensure that the activity is carried out properly, but if a person is deeply involved in a routine activity he is not likely to become involved in creative problem solving. Thus an organization which keeps all its employees submerged in routine is not likely to produce many creative ideas.

Separation from the existing business

Organic structures can result in greater efficiency in meeting change and in higher levels of creativity. In order to allow for the adoption or the natural growth of such a structure in its development team, it often makes sense to separate new product development from the current business management as far as possible, within the context of the company's business and resources. Most companies are organized simply to make and market their current product range and are at their worst when coping with future breadwinners. 'Innovation calls for more intuitive and exploratory problem solving during the initial phase than routine problem solving.'[9] But the tendency is to add new product functions into existing structures without any consideration as to whether the structure can cope with development efficiently. This approach puts new products into an inferior position well behind existing products, but as a specialist role it is sensible to keep development and the existing business apart from each other in terms of organization. A survey by the Retail Outlets Research Unit[10] showed that a higher level of new-brand introductions into test market occurred among companies with separate, long-standing development departments, and a survey of US packaged goods manufacturers[11] indicated that companies with executives employed full-time on development produced 69 per cent more successful new products than companies with executives working only part of their time on this function.

CONCLUSION

The perfect organizational structure for conducting development activities does not exist. As with any other business activity, development work is done by and among people, resulting in some limitations in efficiency whatever structure is adopted. However, 'the choice of structure is a function of the size and resources of the firm, the company objectives, types of product, the industry in which the firm operates and the availability of expert personnel'.[12] Size and complexity, financial strength, the quality and quantity of the manpower available, the products and the degree of marketing orientation required in the market differ from company to company. Circumstances and people vary between companies and the type of organization will need to vary. The important thing is to establish the best possible organization for the situation, to support it, and to allow it to develop in a way which encourages creative innovation.

REFERENCES

1 Jewkes J, Sawers D and Stillerman R, *The Sources of Invention*, MacMillan, 1969.
2 Booz, Allen and Hamilton Inc, *The Management of New Products*, 1966.
3 Levitt T, *Innovation in Marketing*, McGraw Hill, 1962.
4 Christopher M, 'Venture analysis', *Creating and Marketing New Products* (ed Wills G *et al*), Crosby Lockwood Staples, 1973.
5 Randall G, *Managing New Products*, British Institute of Management, 1980.
6 Achilladelis B, Jervis P and Robertson A, *A Study of Success and Failure in Industrial Innovation*, Centre for the Study of Industrial Innovation, University of Sussex, 1972.
7 Burns T and Stalker M, *The Management of Innovation*, Tavistock, 1961.
8 Johne F A, *Industrial Product Innovation: Organisation and Management*, Croom Helm, 1985.
9 Nyström H, *Creativity and Innovation*, John Wiley and Sons 1979.
10 Mandry G D, *New Product Development in the UK Grocery Trade*, Research Paper No 2, Retail Outlets Research Unit, Manchester Business School, 1973.
11 Grayson R A, 'If you want new products you'd better organise to get them', *Marketing in a Changing World* (ed Morin BA), American Marketing Association, 1969.
12 Hisrich R D and Peters M P, *Marketing a New Product*, The Benjamin/Cummings Publishing Co Inc, 1978.

Figure 3.8 *Alternative organizations for development activities*

Organization	Advantages	Disadvantages
Top Management and R and D	(1) Communication direct (2) Action speedy	(1) Not marketing-oriented and consumer needs may be neglected (2) Too much time can be spent on quality control rather than development
New Products Committee	(1) Good communication (2) Action speedy if a small-scale programme	(1) Same disadvantages as above (2) Unwieldy and action difficult if rate of development increases
Product Managers	(1) A marketing-oriented approach (2) No problem of friction with separate group (3) Problem of handing over from one group to another minimized	(1) Development work may be neglected in favour of existing products (2) Line extensions more likely than new ideas (3) New product budgets may be cut to finance problems on existing products
New Products Department	(1) More priority given to new products (2) Responsibility and accountability vested in one group (3) Full-time effort on new products will give the group special expertise	(1) Development may become out of touch with rest of company (2) Line marketing management may be unenthusiastic about transferred new products (3) Aquisitions handled separately
Diversification Department	(1) Same advantages as new products department (2) Development more likely to occur within limits of the corporate plan (3) New products weighed against acquisitions as a development route	(1) Disadvantages of (1) and (2) in new products department
Venture Management	(1) Entrepreneurial spirit leads to action (2) Draws more fully on the company's resources (3) Encourages evaluation of projects (4) Encourages co-operation	(1) Costly in terms of manpower (2) 'Transfer of knowledge' problem if group disbanded at end of development stage (3) Possible lack of objectivity in evaluating own project (4) Primarily for 'given ideas'

Chapter 4 Planning for Development

THE PROBLEM

New product development is so full of uncertainty that most people who have been involved in the work would probably agree that the orderly schemes found in textbooks do not always fit the untidy reality. But 'in so far as a (new product) manager's job is to impose order on chaos and to keep a system moving in an agreed direction he must plan'.[1]

The lack of a planned development policy can often lead to such unsatisfactory situations as the following, which many managers may be familiar with in their companies:

1. Development work begins on a product simply because the Marketing Manager persuades the R & D Manager to authorise work on his pet project. Thus a product prototype is produced without management approval.
2. The decision to launch a new product is made by the Managing Director when he is approached by the Marketing Director over drinks prior to a dinner function. As a result a decision is made which is based on superficial information.
3. Some senior managers turn a project into a 'sacred cow' which no one dare oppose. Eventually this results in the launch of a product without adequate testing and evaluation.

THE DEVELOPMENT PLAN

To avoid such situations the first task for a person heading up the development organization is to establish a firm policy for that development. This policy should arise out of the corporate plan and result in a long-term strategy on where the company is going, instead of individual development decisions being taken on an opportunistic *ad hoc* basis. The purpose of such a policy is simply to define overall objectives, set growth goals and point the way to growth by one of the different development routes. As a result, criteria will be established for search and evaluation and development guided into areas compatible with the company's resources. Although this approach may be regarded as a little ambitious for small companies, the principles involved can be applied in any company situation.

Profit gap analysis

The first step is to establish just where the company is going currently in terms of profits and to see if a gap exists between the desirable profit target that the company can reasonably be expected to make and the level of profits which existing products can contribute to the target (see Figure 4.1). The profit target tends to be a judgement decision based on a desired return on capital (ROC) and the company's level of resources. The contribution made by existing products is arrived at by projecting future profits from, say, the last five years' sales data with due allowance being made for market trends and likely investment. Many companies, in doing such a simple exercise, will find that such a profit gap does indeed exist.

The profit gap itself cannot of course lead to action; it is just a sum of money that does not yet exist. But this sum of money can be subdivided into a number of separate new product projects. Let us say that the gap in Figure 4.1 at 1992 represents £2.5 million. In theory this could be filled by one product or by 10 products of £250,000. On this assumption one can set about establishing the minimum acceptable profit level for a new product that is necessary to make the effort worthwhile. This level of profit will vary, of course, according to the market and the company's resources. The profit gap will also act as a guide to establishing the maximum acceptable payback period, taking into consideration the competitive situation and the average life cycle for products in the market.

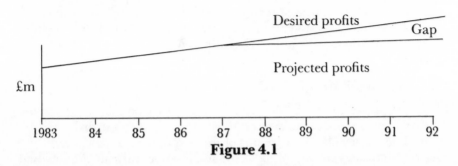

Figure 4.1

The company's resources

Armed with these profit objectives the company can then seek to establish what strengths it possesses which will help it achieve the objectives and what are its major limitations which will set boundaries to the area of search. The principle is that no company is likely to be successful in developing a new product or entering a new market without some firm base in production, marketing or finance. Thus a critical evaluation of strengths and weaknesses should be made in these areas, for example:

1. Marketing resources and skills: the abilities of the marketing team; the company's experience in marketing branded goods; possession or otherwise of established trade names; the company's reputation and image with trade and consumers; the capacity of the salesforce; transport and warehouse facilities and distribution strengths etc.
2. Production resources and skills: production facilities including types of plant, age, capacity and flexibility; factory space, idle plant, seasonality fluctuations; production techniques used; product and design know-how; R and D skills and knowledge of other skills and processes etc.
3. Financial resources: company assets; liquidity; cashflow; access to capital for investment in production facilities and marketing budgets etc.

'By making an audit in this way a good picture can be built up of the company's capabilities.'[2] Thus practical limits are set to the company's development policy and a broad indication of direction is given so that markets may be chosen that are right for the company's mix of skills and resources.

An evaluation of this type may appear to fly in the face of Theodore Levitt's 'Marketing myopia',[3] in that it might lead to a product-oriented or at best a company-oriented development policy rather than one based on consumer needs. But it can also be argued[4] that 'myopia' if taken to an extreme is an over-simplification. Levitt moves an oil company into other forms of energy whereas a wider approach is also relevant. The oil companies have in fact gone vertically into chemicals, fertilizers and plastics, building on their existing strengths rather than entering a field which requires not only new investment but also expertise they do not possess. The business a company is in is the business of meeting its objectives. To do this it has to take into account its strengths and weaknesses.

Selecting markets

The result of the profit gap analysis and the evaluation of resources can be summarized in the form of a checklist. This should contain a minimum acceptable return (preferably expressed on a discounted cash flow (DCF) basis) and maximum acceptable break-even and cumulative break-even points as well as strengths and weaknesses in terms of marketing, production and finance. It is then possible to look at market data and select markets for further investigation as a result of screening them against the checklist. At this stage the markets should not be looked at in depth but considered from the point of view of size, growth prospects etc. There will be a great difference in the amount of data available on different markets but the sort of questions that should be answered, if possible, at this stage are, for example:

1. What is the size of the market, its trends and growth prospects?
2. What are the trends in the life cycles of products in the market?
3. Who competes in the market and what sort of companies are they?
4. In what areas do the existing manufacturers seem most vulnerable?
5. Who are the consumers?
6. What distribution channels are used to reach the consumer?
7. What production facilities would be required?
8. Does seasonality exist?
9. Are there export opportunities?

Sources of information for the market data would include published retail audits and consumer panels; previous consumer research surveys; product tests and advertising tests; trade association statistics; trade magazine articles; market reports from the Economist Intelligence Unit, Mintel, Euromonitor Publications; and Government data such as the Family Expenditure Survey and the Census of Distribution etc. Three reference books in particular – *Sources of UK Marketing Information*,[5] *Principle Sources of Marketing Information*[6] and *The A-Z of UK Marketing Information Sources*[7] – can be of help in this respect as they give comprehensive details of the type of secondary data that is available.

The evaluation of markets not only guides the company in its selection of markets but also helps it to obtain an indication of the best route for development. It should become clearer from this systematic screening procedure whether to search for new markets for existing products, or to develop new products in existing markets or to diversify with new products into new markets. This is of particular relevance when one considers that acquisition is sometimes the answer when diversification is being considered.

A shortlist of markets should result from the screening process and these can then be analysed in depth. Up to this point the analysis has resulted basically in an elimination of impossible markets; now it is more a matter of positive choice. The object previously was to see in which markets the company might be able to introduce new brands if it used all its skills in marketing, production and finance. At this point the aim is to work out precisely in which markets it should start developing a new brand. The work involved is largely an extension of what has been done so far, but in depth, with the objective of determining whether the company might make profits in particular markets. The study involves looking at the environment in general and at markets in particular in order to identify the key factors affecting success and to predict in what ways they might change. It is a matter partly of going through the data already collected and partly of putting together more complete information. Published data may not be enough and it may be necessary to commission special surveys. In general the study should cover such information as, for example:

1. Demographic trends – birth rate, number of marriages.
2. Sociological trends – leisure, convenience, suburbanization, disposable income.
3. Economic – gross national product, economic forecasts, government policies.
4. Market trends – product life cycle, level of consumer penetration of existing products, pricing policies, brand loyalty, distribution channels, 'entry fee' expenditure.
5. Products – plant required, raw material availability.
6. Industry structure – companies in the market, their access to finance, profit levels, possible mergers, products and marketing policies.
7. Technological trends – likelihood of technological change and its effect on the market.

The aim of collecting this kind of 'hard' data is to discover market opportunities. A number of markets are examind in order to see if there is a physical gap which could be filled profitably. The gap might be no more than the fact that there appears room in the market for a product similar to competitors, or it might be a gap resulting from a non-existent category in the range of products available, for example a shampoo with a completely new ingredient. It might be a more fundamental gap in the sense that a specific consumer activity is not adequately catered for. But emerging from this study should be a very small number of markets in which it is reasonable to try and develop a new product.

Assessing demand

However well supplied with such hard data, it is necessary as the final stage in planning before starting to generate ideas, to supplement this type of data with 'soft' data. In this sense, hard data is essentially a case of objective, observable, enumerative information. Soft data is a matter of opinion, attitude and emotion; its role is both complementary and supplementary. The analysis of hard data may indicate market gaps and the possible size of demand. Whether in fact these are gaps and whether there is a potential demand are questions which enumerative research alone cannot answer. The soft data is concerned with the final demand and what it might be in the future in terms of consumer needs, wants and desires. The starting point is current consumer behaviour. *Ad hoc* usage and attitude surveys, group discussions and depth interviews can be used to collect together the basic information and to answer the questions who buys what, when, where and how; who uses what, when, where and how; and most important of all in this context, who thinks what about existing products. From this data, seen in relation to all the other data, one can try and predict future demand and identify where there might be opportunities for a new brand.

CONCLUSION

With the basic groundwork completed, a sense of direction has been given to the development policy. The profit requirements are defined and the boundaries set to the area of search through the selection of markets which are compatible with the company's resources. Thus a firm brief has been established for the creative sourcing of ideas. A brief which in many ways, perhaps, requires as much creative thought in its formulation as the actual generation of ideas.

CASE STUDY

In descriptions of the planning process the reader is often left with the problem of identifying the theory with a practical situation. To illustrate the principles outlined in this chapter a case history of a company in the UK grocery market, where the author was responsible for planning and development is presented for consideration. In the late 1960s, Libby, McNeill and Libby, then a subsidiary of an American parent, had an annual turnover of around £15 million with two-thirds coming from imported products sold under the company's name and the remainder from products manufacturered at its factory in the UK.

Profit gap analysis indicated that over a five-year period, future profits at best would flatten out, as most of the imported products had reached a stage of market saturation and were likely soon to show evidence of declining volume. Sales were also subject to considerable annual fluctuations, a familiar pattern with imported goods that are derived from good or bad harvests abroad. Most of the domestically produced products however still had potential.

From an analysis of its resources the company believed that with its newly acquired marketing team it now possessed some expertise in this area, but the efficiency of the salesforce left a lot to be desired. The salesforce was largely recruited from outside the grocery trade and was unfamiliar with aggressive selling techniques. It was badly organized and without clearly defined priorities. Indeed, it had been unable to achieve a shop distribution above 40 per cent for any product in the range.

However, the company had acquired over the years, through the quality of its products, a good reputation with the trade and an excellent image in the eyes of consumers. Production know-how, within the limited area of existing products, was good and there was some spare capacity on existing machinery, but this capacity was not sufficient to cope with any major success and the type of product that could be produced on existing machinery was limited to a narrow range, the determining factor being the processing requirements. Plans to expand plant facilities were restricted by a high DCF return which was required by the parent. As the company did not possess any specialized R and D staff the skills in this area were very limited.

With such limitations on plant there was a tendency to look towards imported products for expansion, but these had their own problems. Profit margins were low and there was considerable difficulty in obtaining suppliers who could produce exactly what was required and who could guarantee a secure supply. Although internationally the assets of the company were considerable and there was capital available for investment, any plans to extend plant facilities were affected by the high DCF return requirement and any proposals to incur large scale marketing expenditure were inhibited by fear of failure among some of the top managers and the adverse reaction this might bring from the parent company.

As a result of this analysis the company was able to establish firm development objectives. Profit targets and payback periods were set and emphasis laid on the development of domestically produced items in order to reduce the dependence on imported products. This emphasis would not only lead to products with higher margins but should produce more stable and secure profits. Advantage could be taken of existing technical know-how and also of spare plant capacity, thus eventually reducing the share that all products carried of factory fixed overheads.

Because of the investment problems the types of market open for consideration by the company were limited to the range of the available plant. As a temporary solution to extend opportunities it was decided to investigate companies in the UK that could supply products on a co-pack basis. Such products, it was believed, would allow the company a better profit margin than the margins available from imported products. The company already possessed procurement and buying skills gained through its existing imported business activities. In the long term, if a success was achieved with a co-packed item then it could open the way to an extension of the company's own production facilities. Although maximum and minimum profit targets were established, different criteria were used for co-packed products than for own-manufacture products.

One implication of the limitations on production was that development would be confined to products that could be distributed through the existing distribution system using the current salesforce. But before any product could be launched it was felt necessary to give attention to improving salesforce efficiency. A major reorganization took place involving the elimination of many small accounts and the establishment of planned journey cycles and call norms. In addition, a comprehensive training programme was established. Another reorganization that was required before development could take place was to create from the existing quality control staff a nucleus of an R and D team who were later augmented by skilled people from outside the company.

From the results of the evaluation of resources a checklist was created against which markets were screened. Markets were identified against plant capabilities for own-manufacture products but a much wider choice was available for co-packed products. Here, in contrast to own-manufacture, the principle was adopted of identifying the market opportunity first and then finding the co-packer. Previous research data as well as a wide range of government and privately published data were examined and back data from audits and panels were purchased. Once markets had been selected, in-depth analysis was undertaken with an emphasis on the commissioning of qualitative consumer research to help identify opportunities.

So the basic groundwork was laid for the idea generation stage. The result of this development policy over a three-year period was that of the products that reached the market, one domestically produced new product, namely Libby's 'C' drinks, exceeded the £1 million turnover level in its first year of national sale (1972), three co-packed additions to the product range achieved between them £500,000 in turnover, one product failed in test market and two products failed in mini-testing. On the whole this was quite a successful record. But it was also of significance that the company failed to develop a number of interesting ideas which other companies introduced into the market at a later date. There were in 1985 four products with, at a guestimate, around £20 million turnover, with which the company was at one stage concerned but could not produce a satisfactory prototype product. This suggests that one limitation identified at the resources evaluation stage, namely R and D skills, had not been adequately corrected.

REFERENCES

1 Randall G, *Managing New Products*, British Institute of Management, 1980.
2 Oakley M, *Managing Product Design*, Weidenfeld and Nicolson, 1984.
3 Levitt T, 'Marketing myopia', *Harvard Business Review*, July/August 1960.
4 Simmonds K, 'Removing the chains from product strategy', *Journal of Management Studies*, Vol 5, No 1, February 1968.
5 Wills G, *Sources of UK Marketing Information*, 1968.
6 Hull C, *Principle Sources of Marketing Information*, Times Books, 1975.
7 Shaw C (ed), *The A-Z of Marketing Information Sources*, Euromonitor Publications Ltd, 1984.

Figure 4.2 *Flow chart of planning activities*

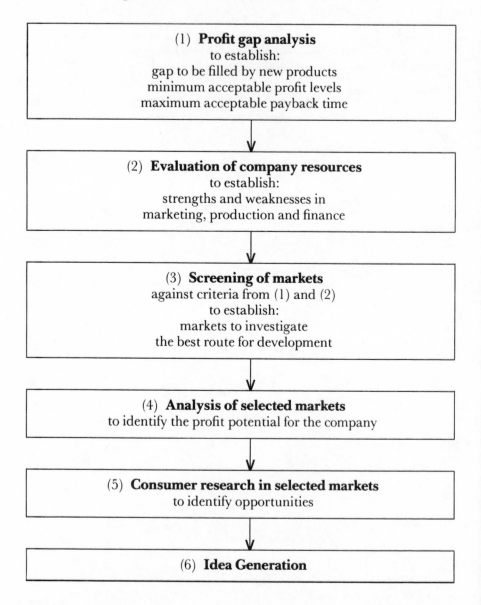

(1) **Profit gap analysis**
to establish:
gap to be filled by new products
minimum acceptable profit levels
maximum acceptable payback time

(2) **Evaluation of company resources**
to establish:
strengths and weaknesses in
marketing, production and finance

(3) **Screening of markets**
against criteria from (1) and (2)
to establish:
markets to investigate
the best route for development

(4) **Analysis of selected markets**
to identify the profit potential for the company

(5) **Consumer research in selected markets**
to identify opportunities

(6) **Idea Generation**

Chapter 5 Ideas for Development

THE PROBLEM

A large amount of evidence has been produced to illustrate the high attrition rate that exists for new product ideas. Perhaps the best documented are the two studies by Booz, Allen and Hamilton Inc in 1966[1] and 1982[2] which illustrate the decay curve for ideas (Figure 5.1). In the 1966 study a total of 58 ideas on average were required to yield one successful product, although this had reduced to seven ideas in the 1982 study. But in both studies only three ideas emerged unscathed through the development stage to enter test market as products.

In a Nielsen study[3] published in 1966 which was limited to grocery, toiletry and household products, only 7 per cent of the total ideas emerged from development to enter test market and over half of these (55 per cent) were unsuccessful in testing.

A Colgate Palmolive study[4] over the period 1959 to 1964 revealed that within that company in the USA there were over 250,000 laboratory experiments resulting in 241 products being selected for product test. Of these, 49 entered test market with only eight being judged successful.

Figures quoted by General Foods of Canada[5] indicate that for every 100 ideas originating within that company 30 survived screening but only six went into test market. And a study[5] of the German pharmaceutical industry showed that of 240 products launched in 1971 only 50 per cent were successful.

Another high failure rate is quoted by Angelus in *Advertising Age*[6] resulting from a study of consumer packaged goods in the USA. Here, from a total of 9,450 products introduced in 1968 almost 80 per cent failed in test market.

Comparison between these studies is difficult because circumstances change from market to market. Moreover a product in test market is easy to identify, but what constitutes a development idea is another matter. In studies of this type, an idea for some companies may be a raw idea before

49

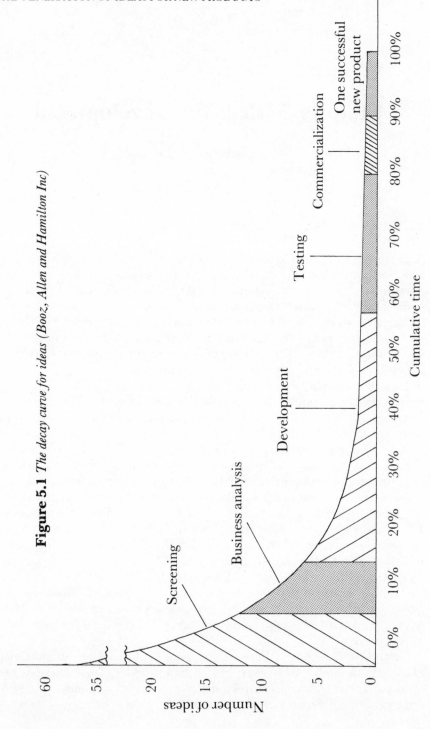

Figure 5.1 *The decay curve for ideas (Booz, Allen and Hamilton Inc)*

preliminary screening has taken place and for others it may not be recognized as a development idea until after this stage or even until after analysis in depth of practicality and potentiality. The number of ideas necessary to produce a new product must therefore remain an open question although it can be recognized that a high attrition rate exists.

There is no problem in evaluating the success of new products after national launch as such products are easily identifiable and here the decay curve appears to continue at a fairly rapid rate. In a study[7] of the UK grocery trade, Mandry shows that one in four products launched nationally in 1966 were withdrawn by 1970. A J Walter Thompson Ltd study[8] in the UK revealed that of 294 new products launched in the grocery market from 1954 to 1960, a total of 49 per cent had been withdrawn by 1964. In a Swedish study[9] of 616 brands introduced in 1950 only 187 were still on the market in 1960. Finally, a summary by Crawford (1983)[10] of every study of success/failure that had been cited in new product literature since World War II indicated that 25 per cent of all industrial products and 30 to 35 per cent of consumer products fail in the market place.

PRODUCT LIFE CYCLES

That so many products are withdrawn after a relatively short period on the market illustrates the short life cycles that many products now suffer. The continuing high rate of technological change in the second half of this century is no doubt a major influence on these life cycles. New technologies not only bring one innovation to supplant another, either in product design or manufacturing process, but technology also has an indirect influence. It has led to greater economic wealth and higher income levels which have affected product choice. Higher incomes in turn have brought leisure and money to travel and this, with new forms of mass communication, particularly television, has made the average consumer a little more sophisticated and more prepared to try things that are new. Also, higher income levels for the young has meant the emergence of a new market with new needs and often a fashion-oriented approach to products. As a result of all these factors, consumer needs, tastes and attitudes have tended to change quickly. Moreover the increase in marketing orientation in the business world has led to more competitive markets, so that a manufacturer seldom enjoys the fruits of his discovery alone for very long and with this knowledge he is continuously on the look out for opportunities to improve his product and even to supplant it with another.

The emergence of the young market and the creation of a more catholic population generally influences the speed with which new products are accepted, thus affecting the length of their life cycles. The theory of diffusion[11] first advanced by researchers at the Iowa State University suggests that innovations tend to diffuse in a consistent manner following the curve of the product life cycle, in which the first trial purchases are made by the venturesome 'innovators' who tend to be young, cosmopolitan and of high income. Further research[12] has indicated that the characteristics of the innovators vary according to product but it would appear reasonable to assume that many products are first 'discovered' by this group of purchasers. The last 30 years have seen the growth of a substantial group of people with these characteristics and the rise of a more cosmopolitan and a wealthier population as a whole. This has no doubt resulted in the quicker adoption of new products generally and consequently shorter product life cycles.

A PROGRAMME FOR DEVELOPMENT

With shorter life cycles it is essential that, if a company is to improve or even maintain its position, a system or basic set of principles for developing new products is adopted. Without such a system a company may eventually find itself with a product range consisting of nothing but 'yesterday's breadwinners', to use the now famous terminology of Peter Drucker.[13] An example is quoted by Parker[14] of a large company that saw its percentage of successful innovations rise from 10 to 50 per cent after the adoption of a careful, systematic programme. The 'classic' programme for development as detailed by Booz, Allen and Hamilton Inc,[1] Pessemier[15] and others consists of six steps. These are:

1. Idea generation.
2. Screening.
3. Business analysis.
4. Development.
5. Testing.
6. Commercialization.

IDEA GENERATION

'Marketing's most difficult task is the finding, testing and launching of profitable new products', is how the A C Nielsen Co Ltd[16] has referred to this programme for development. Perhaps the most difficult step in the programme is the first − idea generation. It is certainly the most important, if only because the remaining steps just cannot take place without ideas to progress. Yet many companies in their development programmes appear not to appreciate the overriding importance of this stage. The programme is oriented to other stages. Emphasis is laid, say, on the screening or the testing of 'given' ideas, without enough thought being given to ensure that disciplined procedures are developed to make certain that ideas are available for the screening and testing stages. The effectiveness of the other steps is obviously limited by the number and quality of the product ideas that are discovered.

A suggestion has been made that 'the generation of ideas is a relatively easy task and certainly not as difficult as is often made out'. The author of this statement[17] cites as an example that most individuals are capable of coming up with an idea if an hour or so is spent in considering a given product field. Anyone who has sat in on numerous think-tanks and discussions will appreciate that this is a somewhat naive attitude. Certainly any individual is capable of coming up with an idea or two, but unfortunately in reality most of these ideas are either lacking in potential, impractical to produce or outside the company's terms of reference. This is especially true of the ideas that arise without the aid of disciplined procedures. Any individual can think up a new product idea like 'canned boiled eggs' but no company has been able, or felt inclined, to introduce it on to the market.

An approach which has been often used to cover the idea generation stage and one which many companies still follow is a procedure of random idea submission, in which ideas are left to the people directly concerned in product development, with occasional requests to company personnel as a whole. Although this may have a semblance of an approach it is basically a haphazard procedure which relies mainly on chance. A system is required in which ideas are generated through an organized network with a central collection point. This network should cover both inside and outside the company and utilize a variety of idea collection methods and techniques.

In a study of 11 companies in Sweden a total of 54 out of 91 ideas came from internal sources, although externally obtained ideas were associated with more successful products.[18] The large number of ideas that are required to find one successful product suggests that to become a successful developer of new products one must first become a successful developer of new ideas. In the study[7] conducted by Mandry, one characteristic of companies successful in development was their ability to generate ideas. His 'innovative companies' averaged 65 ideas each in a year whereas the average for 'non-innovative companies' was only 35. On the other hand his innovative companies do not appear to possess a superiority in screening and in test marketing. Such a superiority should be revealed by a higher level of rejection of ideas and a higher level of failure in test market respectively, but the study does not indicate this. So in general it appears that idea generation, if conducted efficiently, is the stage in the development process which is most likely to lead to success.

In spite of this, the Mandry study suggests idea generation does not appear to receive enough attention. Only 16 per cent on average of a company's market research development budget for both innovative and non-innovative companies is spent on this stage. This compares with 22 per cent on concept testing and 24 per cent on product tests. Moreover this is from a budget which is small, representing on average only 0.9 per cent of turnover.[7]

CONCLUSION

Although a considerable number of ideas appear to be required for successful product development, this is not to suggest that the sheer quantity of ideas – good or bad – should be regarded obsessively by companies as a new yardstick for measuring performance. What is important is the search for those few significant, potentially profitable ideas. For method applied to idea generation is not a magic formula. There is, in the final analysis, no substitute for creativity. But if one concentrates only on quality it is not easy to forecast in advance which techniques will necessarily produce the best results (although this aspect is examined in Chapter 7). There is no guarantee that concentration on a few favourite techniques to produce only quality ideas will achieve the desired objective.

It has been suggested[19] that the best ideas arise from highly selective probing into the market rather than from the production of a flood of ideas, most of which will be impractical. Further, that this probing should be conducted by senior marketing management whose creative and intellectual judgement, based on a working knowledge of consumer behaviour will lead to potential growth opportunities being identified.

There is every reason to rely on senior marketing management as a prime source of ideas but this viewpoint appears to suggest that in all companies marketing personnel are the sole depositories of creative and intellectual judgement. Creativity cannot be restricted in such a simple way. Creative ideas can be produced from many sources, in many ways, involving different types of people. The secret of successful idea generation may be to start by looking at all sources but quickly to drop the ones which are least fruitful for a particular company. New ideas can arrive from a wide variety of sources and it is perhaps safer initially to keep them all open, with the objective of looking after the quantity and allowing the quality to look after itself.

REFERENCES

1 Booz, Allen and Hamilton Inc, *The Management of New Products*, 1966.
2 Booz, Allen and Hamilton Inc, *New Product Management for the 1980s*, 1982.
3 A C Nielsen Inc, *How to Strengthen Your Product Plan*, 1966.
4 Van Camp R W, 'Essential elements for new product success', *New Product Development* (ed Eastlack J O Jnr), American Marketing Association, 1968.

5 Andrews B, *Creative Product Development*, Longman, 1975.
6 Angelus T L, 'Why do most new products fail', *Advertising Age*, 24 March 1969.
7 Mandry G D, *New Product Development in the UK Grocery Trade*, Research Paper No 2, Retail Outlets Research Unit, Manchester Business School, 1973.
8 Dunbar D S, 'New lamps for old', *The Grocer*, 3 April 1965.
9 Leduc R, *How to Launch a New Product*, Crosby Lockwood, 1966.
10 Crawford C M, *New Products Management*, Irwin, 1983.
11 Rogers E., *The Diffusion of Innovations*, Collier-MacMillan, 1962.
12 Donnelly J H and Etzel H J, 'Degrees of product newness and early trial', *Journal of Marketing Research*, August 1973.
13 Drucker P, *Managing for Results*, Pan, 1964.
14 Parker R C, *Guidelines for Product Innovation*, British Institute of Management, 1980.
15 Pessemier E A, *New Product Decisions – An Analytical Approach*, McGraw Hill, 1966.
16 A C Nielsen Co Ltd, *The Realities of New Product Marketing*, Nielsen Researcher, Jan/Feb 1970.
17 Midgley D F, *Innovation and New Product Marketing*, Croom Helm, 1977.
18 Nyström H, *Creativity and Innovation*, John Wiley and Sons, 1979.
19 Pollitt S, 'A practical approach to new products and new concepts', *Admap*, March 1970.

Figure 5.2 *Flow chart of development activities*

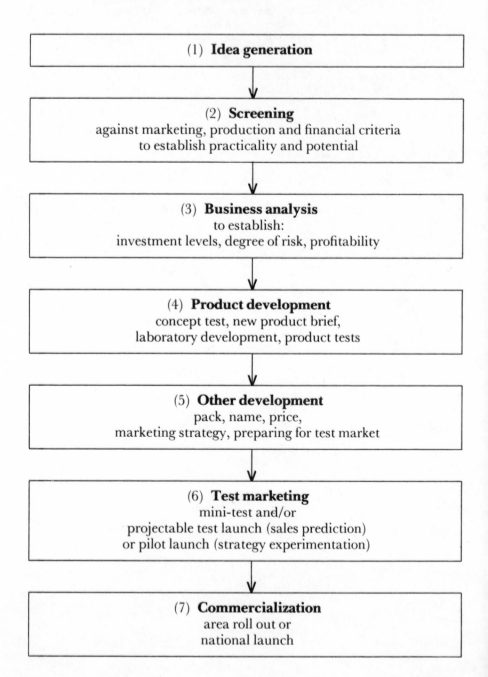

Chapter 6 The Techniques for Idea Generation

INTRODUCTION

Once an organizational structure has been established and the planning framework completed, then a company can begin seriously to generate ideas for new products. This is not an easy task, as outlined in the previous chapter, and there appears to be a need to use as many sources and techniques as possible. But the manager directly responsible for new products could spend many months patiently sifting the published literature on new products in an attempt to gather together a reasonable range that could be used. The purpose of Chapter 6 is to make this easy; it contains descriptions of over 60 sources and techniques that can be used in the search for new products. With the majority, the description will be enough to enable the technique to be directly applied within the company. Where it is felt by a manager that additional information could be of help, the references at the end of the chapter and the publications listed in Appendix 2 will be of assistance.

IDEAS FROM OVERSEAS

Markets abroad can prove a fruitful source of ideas for new products. For example, Cadbury's 'Smash' is based on a US formula and Crawford's 'Tuc' biscuit is of Belgian origin. The idea for Lever Brothers' 'Shield' and 'Wisk' also came from the US, while 'Jif' came from France. Many other well-known products such as 'St Ivel Gold', Rowntree's 'Texan Bar' and Findus 'Pancakes' also originated abroad. The highly developed markets are of course in the USA and Europe and these are the most likely sources of ideas. It has been said that the UK market follows the trend established in the USA with a time lag of five to 10 years (for example, cordless electrical appliances followed this pattern). But there is no natural law that products from other markets will necessarily transplant and where they do, product modifications are frequently necessary. Foreign markets can be monitored in several ways.

Travelling abroad

Visits càn be made to overseas markets in search of new ideas, with a representative of the company making a planned tour visiting stores and/or exhibitions. It is important that an experienced (and creative) person makes these visits rather than a junior, and that the visits are an end in themselves and not tacked on as something additional (and inferior) to a visit arranged for another purpose. The visit is made not just to look for established products which could be launched directly into the home market. Seeing products in a new environment can spark off ideas, through the operation of chance, which bear no relationship to the product causing the stimulus. Arrangements can also be made to visit manufacturers abroad with a view to obtaining products on a co-pack basis.

Examining foreign literature

Apart from visiting markets, ideas can also be obtained seated at one's desk in the office by examining overseas publications. Both the editorials and the advertisements in women's and general interest magazines and trade journals can be of interest, as well as sales brochures and trade fair catalogues. The American women's magazine *McCalls* is well known in this context as is *Marketing Communications* (formerly *Printers Ink*), which reviews new products launched in the US market. The OEEC publishes a bulletin called *European Technical Digest* which lists major new European products and technical developments.

From time to time certain companies, usually marketing consultants or research companies, make it their business to collect information on new products that have been launched in various overseas countries and to make regularly published reports available to manufacturers on a subscription basis. Often the publication only lasts for a year or two and then ceases because of a fall in membership subscription. Then later another company will start a similar publication. These also can be useful sources of new product ideas. Currently available are the new product reports covering various areas of the world from ICS Ltd, *New Product News* from Dancer Fitzgerald Sample Inc in the USA and *New Products in Grocers* from the consultants KAE in the UK.

Employing freelance 'scouts'

It is also sometimes possible to employ 'product scouts' abroad. The scout could be an independent consultant or a representative of a foreign (though not competitive) manufacturer, paid on a fee basis to report on new products.

Information from subsidiaries or sister companies

The large international company with foreign subsidiaries can establish a system whereby products new to each subsidiary (and also possibly competitors' products too) are reported to head office. Here the reports are collated in a newsletter which is sent to all subsidiaries. If a product is developed by, say, the Australian company and the UK company thinks it could be launched into their own market, then it is easy for them to obtain the technical know-how and the marketing launch experience of the Australian company to guide them. For instance, the Nestlé Co distribute monthly to all their subsidiaries from the head office in Vevey, Switzerland, a publication called *Communication Marketing* which contains details of new products developed by its companies operating in all parts of the world. Further details can then be obtained from the market concerned by an interested subsidiary.

It should also be mentioned that advertising agencies, where they have an international network of branches, can also be used to obtain information and samples of products.

SPECIALIZED MARKET RESEARCH TECHNIQUES

A number of specialized market research techniques can be used in the process of idea generation. The techniques examined in this section are all derived from 'personal construct theory' and are rather complex (and expensive) to carry out. More standard consumer market research techniques are dealt with later in this chapter.

The repertory grid technique

This is a technique which has a wide range of applications.[1] It is of value in new product development because it can give data concerning individual consumer attitudes towards the field under investigation and thus by inference help in finding gaps which new products can fill. Basic to the technique is presenting individuals with brands in threes and asking in which ways two are similar and the third different. Ultimately an exhaustive list of ways of looking at the product type can emerge.

Historically, the repertory grid emerged as a procedure attached to a formal framework called personal construct theory which was published by an American psychologist, G A Kelly. The theory sets out the notion that man codifies his observations into a framework of personal 'constructs'. A construct is different from a concept in that whereas the latter is a label or a group name, for example strong beers, a construct is specifically required to have a dimensionality. Strong beers exist at one end of a dimension which in construct terms would be strong-weak.

The procedures for the grid runs on the following lines. A list is drawn up of all the brand names in the field under study which are transferred on to cards, each card carrying the name of a single brand. Interviews are carried out individually with each respondent by the administering interviewer/ psychologist who presents the entire pack of cards to the respondent and asks him to remove any brand with which he is totally unfamiliar. Next, three cards are selected according to a predetermined randomization procedure and the respondent asked in what way any two of the three brands are similar to each other and different from the third. Having elicited the first construct in this way the respondent is asked to sort the remaining cards according to the construct produced. The respondent is then handed a different set of three cards and the instruction repeated, that is to think of any way in which any two are similar to each other and different from the third. However, the respondent is additionally instructed not to repeat a response that has already been given and in this way a new construct is obtained. The sorting procedure is then repeated for this new construct. The interview continues until the respondent has exhaused his repertoire of constructs relating to the field by which time the grid, representing that particular respondent's attitudes, will include ratings of all products under study on all constructural dimensions.

Examination of a number of grids derived from a series of interviews reveals that while individual respondents have their own pattern of constructs there is a considerable degree of overlap, so that by the time 20 to 40 such interviews have been carried out no new constructs can be obtained from any further interviews. Analysis of the grids can then indicate common personal constructs which are couched in the vocabulary of the consumer and not a vocabulary which has been imposed on him. Constructs set out in the form of bi-polar scales can present dimensions which the inarticulate might not otherwise have been able to express spontaneously.

The stimulus cards which normally carry brand names may be replaced with photographs, prototype products or actual products, especially in development studies for food products.

Analysis of the grids can reveal associations between brands and constructs, which provides material concerning consumer attitudes on which the creative mind can work. The grid analysis need not necessarily be complex but it is inevitably laborious when carried out by hand and simple computerized routines may be developed.

The St James model

With this technique the repertory grid is incorporated into a three-stage programme:

1. Repertory grids: interviews to explore consumer attitudes on a construct basis towards products in a given market category.
2. Factor analysis: small-scale study to organize, screen and reduce the list of attribute constructs derived from the previous stage.
3. Large-scale survey: using the shortlist from the second stage in which existing brands and an 'ideal brand' (built up from the shortlist) are rated according to preference.

The aims of the St James model are to find out what consumers rate as the most important attributes and to discern how the characteristics of existing brands compare with the 'ideal brand'. This helps identify market segments which require special product features.

Gap analysis

This technique offers another formalized approach to the identification of new product opportunities based on Kelly's theory of personal constructs, in which a perceptual model of the market from the consumer's viewpoint is constructed in order to see where gaps in the market may exist. Having isolated gaps a creative team can then attempt to produce new product ideas to meet areas of unfulfilled needs.

Basic to the technique, as in the repertory grid, is the tenet that perception has a dimensionality, that objects are perceived along spectra such as thick-thin, weak-strong etc. Consequently a picture of the market structure along such spectra can be built up.

The approach starts with a qualitative examination of the kind of attitudes that surround the products in the market. Depth interviews can be used for this purpose. Such attitudes form the basis of the spectra and can be product attributes, users, types of use, associations or indeed anything that discriminates between the brands in the market. For example, with soft drinks the spectra could include: sweet-tart; slimming-fattening; nourishing-not nourishing; healthy-not healthy; enjoyable-not enjoyable; expensive-inexpensive; hot-cold; suitable for children-not suitable, etc. The outcome of this stage is a comprehensive list of bi-polar attitude statements. These are then edited and pruned into seven-point scales. The next stage involves quantification, and opinions are obtained from a sample of consumers as to their rating of existing products on the selected bi-polar attitude scales (see Figure 6.1).

This is the basic data for the gap analysis programme. It is possible to examine the attitude factors one at a time and identify unoccupied spaces on each bi-polar scale, but this can be time consuming if a large number of scales is involved. Perhaps the easiest way of handling this manually would be to reproduce each scale on transparent film and place the scales together as on a series of overlays. But the technique can be extended to a large number of dimensions and it is easier to use a computer to carry out gap analysis involving a high number of variables.

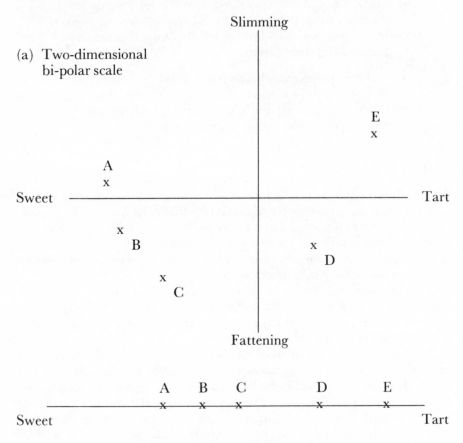

(a) Two-dimensional bi-polar scale

(b) One-dimensional bi-polar scale

Figure 6.1

To discourage useless results it is possible to impose limits on each variable. These limits can be defined by existing products that nobody wants, say, a football-sized aspirin. Thus no new product may be bigger or smaller, sweeter or less sweet, cheaper or more expensive than those already marketed.

Judgement can be used as to whether the gaps identified represent consumer needs. However, in the technique[2] devised by Clemens and Thornton at McCann Erickson, the gaps are tested on consumers on the basis that they may be so numerous that some form of objective screening is necessary. Each gap has three or four concepts developed for it, creatively represented both visually and verbally on small press advertisement sized cards. Similarly, the concepts for existing products are placed on cards. These are then presented to a sample of consumers and repertory grid procedures utilized to discern whether the concepts developed do in fact represent the gaps for which they were conceived and whether they are meaningful to consumers. The concepts which emerge are then screened at a theatre test. The audience is shown slides on which the product concepts are typified, together with slides for existing products and asked to select which product they would like to win as a prize in a draw that is being held in the theatre.

A simplified version of gap analysis can be done, in which greater reliance is placed on subjective judgement. Attempts are made to discover attitudes to brands either from existing market research or from small-scale qualitative studies and then the positions of various brands are plotted on a judgement basis. The gaps isolated are, of course, only as good as the judgement exercised and as a result more responsibility is placed on subsequent research to check whether the assumptions on which the concepts are based are valid.

There is more than one way to use gap analysis. Classic market gaps can be looked for, that is spaces on the grid of bi-polar scales where there are no existing products. Also one can look for different ways of combining characteristics of existing products into a new combination. In particular the characteristics of the two or three most successful products can be analysed to try and discover the common threads, with a view to keeping these major features but changing one or two elements to make a distinctive new product.

Gap analysis is based on the belief that opportunities exist in any market at any time if only one cares to identify them. It is a logical technique which automatically can produce novel items. It has been criticized on the grounds that, in spite of the time and cost involved, one may produce novel but unmarketable items. Certainly the results can never be better than the original data and some ingenuity may be required in interpreting the findings.

Non-metric mapping

This technique, which is of more recent origin, is a simpler version of gap analysis. It requires respondents to rank products according to their preferences or perceived similarities or dissimilarities. A 'map' of these products can be produced which best describes these perceptions on the basis of the distribution of the products in space. For example, if

THE GENERATION OF IDEAS FOR NEW PRODUCTS

respondents were required to arrange a selection of cheeses in pairs so that each pair is most similar to each other and not as similar to a cheese in any other pair, the result could be: cheddar/cheshire; cheese slices/Dairylea; stilton/Danish blue; camembert/gruyère; and so on. Alternatively, cheeses could be ranked individually according to preference instead and similar information would be obtained.[3]

This raw data is then subjected to a computer program which 'maps' the products in space. In effect, the computer examines the rank orders and produces distance maps in dimensions on the basis of the extent to which every combination of pairs (or single items if ranked individually according to preference) is sees as 'close to' or 'far away from' every other combination of pairs. In practice what is provided is a multi-dimensional map with products on a number of dimensions of a market at the distances from each other as perceived by consumers (see Figure 6.2). The arrangement of the products has to be interpreted by those examining the 'maps' and it is necessary to identify the number of meaningful dimensions, the relative importance and meaning of each dimension and the distribution of the products along these dimensions.

The technique aims not just to produce a gap but the location which is best preferred by respondents and allows prediction of how consumers would react to any arbitrarily located new product. The ideas generated by this method therefore, have a certain degree of viability already associated with them. Thus the technique can be valuable in helping to identify new product opportunities, although it can be criticized on the grounds that the ideas produced may tend to be modifications of existing products rather than product innovations.

Unlike other approaches to perceptual mapping, the basic input is very simple research data; the sophistication comes in the data processing and in the interpretation of the results. It is of course possible to do further research in order to obtain consumer interpretation of the groupings produced by the method rather than relying on interpretation by management.

Typically, a non-metric mapping study is conducted on relatively small samples of approximately 25 respondents. This is more to do with the complexity of the computer programming, where there are now a number of developed programs available, than with any real assessment of relevant sample size. As a result it is claimed that the technique is cheaper and quicker than gap analysis, which is more complex and time consuming in research terms. However, because of the element of sophistication in the data processing, non-metric mapping studies are usually carried out by a consultancy specializing in the technique.

Figure 6.2 *A non-metric map of the UK cheese market*[3]
(ranked according to preference)

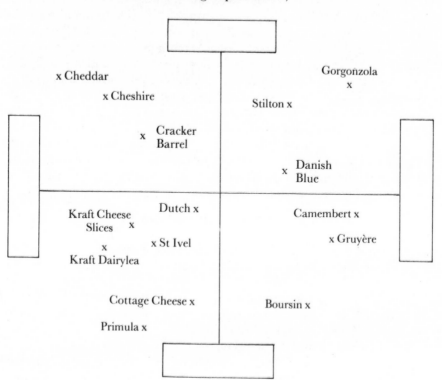

IDEAS FROM COMPANY EMPLOYEES

People engaged in marketing, sales and market research are naturally more aware of the need for new products than employees from other departments. Yet anyone can have ideas: someone on the shop floor, a clerk dealing with letters of complaint from customers and others within the company, are all in working environments which can encourage problem-solving creativity. It is important to regard the whole of the company's employees as a potential source of new product ideas. To take full advantage of this source it is essential to state the company's new product goals in such a way that all employees are in a position to make a positive contribution. They should be made aware of the company's strengths and weaknesses and the resulting objectives in relation to new products. As a result employees will have the necessary background data on which to base their thinking. This will inevitably cut down the number of completely impractical ideas that could be suggested. There are several methods of obtaining ideas on a formalized basis.

A company suggestion scheme

Company employees can be asked for their ideas, which have to be suggested by a deadline date. An announcement could be made in the staff newsletter, for instance, or a memorandum issued. Background information should be given of course – company objectives, the nature of the competition and anything that can inspire practical ideas. Staff could be encouraged to jot down their ideas in a notebook so that they do not get forgotten. This whole process helps to create a climate favourable to the production of new ideas. However, a long enough period should be allowed as creativity does demand time.

To make the process more continuous a suggestion scheme can be established on a permanent basis. To be effective it must be easy to submit ideas and the scheme must appear fair. Several factors should be considered in order to facilitate this:

1. A special form could be made available at some central point, say reception.
2. Suggestions should go through one point of contact.
3. An acknowledgement should be sent to the person submitting the idea.
4. If the suggestion is not accepted, the reason should be given in writing directly to the person concerned. There is nothing worse for morale than a cold rejection slip.
5. A scheme of awards should be clearly stated.
6. Ideas'should be reviewed by a committee and not by an individual if the scheme is to appear fair.

Overall, the scheme must be handled with skill if it is to be effective and if the danger of bad relations developing between an employee and the company is to be avoided.

A survey by the National Industrial Conference Board as early as 1966, which embraced 86 companies in the USA, showed that 60 per cent of these companies gave special rewards to what might be termed 'employee-inventors'. Most gave small sums, although 11 per cent allowed royalties. It is possibly worthwhile offering substantial rewards. In Switzerland, Sweden and West Germany the law requires that royalties be paid to employee-inventors, which does appear to stimulate invention as these three countries have the largest number of patent applications.

R and D staff working on their own initiative

R and D personnel are of course part of the development team and most of their work should follow a marketing brief which has been based on research into consumer needs. However, it is important to allow R and D staff some time of their own to pursue their own ideas. Roberts[4] quotes several studies, beginning with Pelz in the mid-60s, that demonstrates that diversity of work activity tends to improve the idea generating performance of technical people. Not only can this affect the quality of all R and D work in that it gives greater job satisfaction to the personnel involved, but 'self-starter' work of this nature can also lead to marketable ideas. A lot of valueless products remote from consumer requirements might also be produced, but on the evidence of a survey conducted by Greenhalgh,[5] a substantial number of acceptable new products (14 per cent) resulted from the independent creative flair of R and D staff. Another study[6] showed that such well-known products as Aspro Clear and Crown Silk Vinyl Emulsion Paint originated in this way.

An employee panel

Panels of about a dozen employees can be established, perhaps including also members of the families of those selected. The panels are utilized as discussion or brainstorming groups. Two or three panels can be set up and the membership changed after six or so meetings. Change serves not only to bring fresh minds to the problems in hand but also helps create more employee involvement in the development process generally.

Invention groups

As an extention of the panel, an invention group can be established, consisting of employees chosen from a cross-section of departments. The group is sent away outside the company, perhaps to a country inn, for one day a month for a period of around six months and charged with the task of producing ideas for new products. The purpose of spending time away is to produce an atmosphere of informality and relaxation free from the constraints which can arise within the company building itself. The invention group is a technique which was developed and used successfully by Colgate Palmolive in the USA.

Think tanks

A management-oriented variant on the invention group is the think tank, whose membership is confined to marketing personnel or to senior managers representing the departments who are directly concerned in the innovation process. Outsiders such as advertising agency executives may also be enrolled as members in order to help avoid introverted company thinking.

Naturally enough, many products originate from marketing people discussing opportunities in this way. McVities United Biscuit, Quaker Hot Oat Cereal and Beechams Pure and Simple Skin Cream and Lotion are examples of what must be in reality an almost exhaustless list.

Job rotation

Another attempt to obtain a fresh approach is by means of job rotation, in which a member of another department is seconded to the marketing development team for a short period of time. This could be established on a permanent basis with one person coming in to replace another at the end of a set time period. Each person seconded to the team would join fully in all activities but his specific concern would be idea generation.

Circulation sheets

Although it can be simple to operate this technique to elicit ideas from employees, it is virtually impossible for a scheme of awards to be incorporated unless it is made on a group basis. The brief is stated on, say, the first page of a folder which is circulated twice round a group of people within the company. The folder passes from one person to another with each recipient being asked to add his own ideas on the problem, the comments appearing anonymously. The folder needs to circulate twice in order to give the opportunity for each person involved to improve on his original suggestion, taking into consideration the ideas sparked off by others. A great deal of worthless material is bound to result, but there may be one or more good ideas resulting from this very inexpensive method.

Past ideas and projects

Examining files dealing with old ideas and projects which have not been pursued can sometimes be of value, as it was for Birds Eye Foods with the introduction of their frozen doughnut product. Ideas may have been hastily and wrongly assessed or even have been ahead of their time, with circumstances now changed. An old idea may also have the effect of sparking off a new idea worthy of development.

To increase productivity from any method which involves company employees, it is possible to provide short internal courses in creative thinking. This was done at the A C Spark Plug Division of General Motors in the USA, and research was conducted to measure its effect. The result was that during the year following the training the number of contributions made to the company suggestion scheme increased by over 40 per cent.

IDEAS FROM COMPANY SALESFORCE

The salesforce may be looked upon as a special group of company employees because they are the ones who are nearest to the consumer. In continuous contact with the trade, who in turn are in direct contact with consumers, a salesman is likely to develop ideas for new products. As with other company employees he should be made aware of the company's objectives in relation to development, as this will act as a framework for his personal thoughts on the subject. In order to stimulate and collect these thoughts a number of techniques can be adopted.

Contests

New product contests can be held. For, say, a three-month period indirect pressure is applied through the lure of prizes that can be obtained for the submission of acceptable ideas.

Report forms

This method can be utilized in a mandatory fashion on the basis of, say, one idea per week from each salesman over a specific period of time. Space for ideas is allowed on the call report form thus aiming at the maximum number of ideas, however wild. Alternatively the process could be less commanding, with a special form completed each month/quarter giving details of new product ideas, competitive activities, market conditions etc, in a sort of 'field intelligence' report. Whichever method is used, however, it is necessary to exercise firm control. Otherwise this aspect of form filling will tend to be neglected under the pressure of more immediate daily routine business.

Ideas at sales meetings

Ideas can be encouraged in an organized way as part of a sales meeting. In addition, brainstorming sessions may be held among groups of salesmen. Ideally such sessions would be an end in themselves with a group called specifically to a central point. However, all marketing personnel are aware of the problems concerned with taking salesmen off the road and it may be advisable to run a brainstorming session after a normal sales meeting — although not ideal it may prove more practicable. (Brainstorming as a technique is discussed later in this chapter.)

Group discussions and depth interviews

These research techniques, considered later in this chapter, may also be used involving selected members of the salesforce.

Salesmen as a whole are enthusiastic about selling. Naturally, in order to sell more they want to sell products which people desire. Therefore they are bound to develop ideas about products, providing a useful source which can be of value to a company if an effort is made to organize the flow of ideas. Many companies have had numerous ideas from the salesforce which have resulted in successful products. However, particular care should be taken in screening, as enthusiasm can lead to ideas which are impractical for technical and financial reasons and also to opinions which may be prejudiced by bad sales locally.

IDEAS FROM OUTSIDE THE COMPANY

Inventors

A direct approach to seeking ideas is to advertise for 'inventors' to submit their proposals to the company. Many managers would probably be afraid to undertake such a step, visualizing their head office lobbies filled with hordes of inventors wasting valuable time. No doubt many useless offerings would be presented but one solid idea would make this risk worthwhile. For example, the 'roll-on' idea for the original Bristol Myers Ban roll-on deodorant came from a private inventor outside the company.

One other fear may arise for managers from the fact that the respective rights in the idea may raise legal complications. Obviously a company must protect itself if it is exposed to a new product concept which is simply an inventor's brainstorm without full documentation or a working model. With such ideas and also with those that are fully documented, some legal arrangement must be made before further development work is undertaken.

Patents

The *Official Journal (Patents)* is the register of all new patent applications in the UK. There are equivalent publications abroad such as the *Official Gazette* of the US Patent Office. The main problem in relation to patents is that there are so many registered that pinpointing those of relevance can present difficulties. One way is to limit the search to patents that have recently expired. A private watchmaker took out a patent for a self-winding watch as early as 1923 and when the patent expired several Swiss manufacturers produced and launched models. In addition, those that have been recently registered could be included in the search. This will enable the possible exploitation of relevant ideas not covered by registration now and perhaps the generation of fresh concepts arising from new patents but not covered in their registration.

Licensing

One way of exploiting a patent that is held by another manufacturer is to arrange to develop the product and then to sell it under licence. It is easier of course to sell under licence an already developed product that another manufacturer is currently selling in his own market. This has become quite common in the UK beer market over the past two decades, with several well-known lagers and also the sale of Colt 45 by Courage under licence from the National Brewing Corporation of Baltimore, USA. A study of products sold abroad would be a first step to take and one could even advertise for products in such publications as the *Wall Street Journal* and the *Financial Times*. Even in one's own national market, a small company with insufficient resources or a large company who does not wish to sell products outside its main area of interest may be open to an arrangement being made.

Potential licensers are not only likely to look for a satisfactory fee but also for long-term profits. Thus the licence contract, as well as protecting the licenser by providing for royalty adjustments if sales exceed expectations, should also protect the licensee from incurring unexpected costs arising from a need to redesign the product extensively in order to adapt it to his own market. Negotiating licence contracts is a special skill and often requires outside legal help. In order to ensure success once the venture has commenced, frequent visits on a two-way basis are advisable so that the 'tricks of the trade' with regard to the manufacture and sale of the product may be fully understood by the licensee.

Joint ventures

An alternative to a licensing agreement is for the two companies concerned to share the risks and the profits in a joint venture. These arrangements often follow the pattern that as 'capital' one company brings its product and manufacturing facilities to the venture and the other brings its marketing organization and market contacts. Friction between the two companies can be a problem and perhaps the best basis for a joint venture is where the two companies are in different countries, so that the partner possessing the product is a long way removed from the other's market. The success of Rank Xerox which was set up by the Rank Organisation in the UK and the Haloid Corporation in the USA to develop the Xerox process outside North America illustrates this point.

For the company that is diversifying, both joint ventures and licensing arrangements save time and money. But the profits have to be shared and there is a danger that considerable long-term success could lead the diversifier into regretting not having spent the time and money to develop his own product.

Acquisitions

A logical extension to the joint venture is for the diversifier to acquire the company with the product. If the product is already well established this can bring rapid entry into a market with a known volume of profit. Obtaining a product by acquisition is really an alternative to internal new product development and as with internal development any ideas concerning acquisitions should be carefully screened. Indeed, the steps involved are basically similar in that the company should identify areas of interest, screen these areas, investigate possible companies, negotiate terms and finally organize the acquisition into an effective operating entity. An acquisition policy should be integrated with internal development and not be conducted as a haphazard, unrelated activity. Both offer alternative routes with neither one excluding the other.

The cost of a failed acquisition is high in both financial and human terms and unlike a new product it cannot be tested first of all in the market place. Many acquisitions fail because they are seen in isolation and not as part of an overall growth strategy. To minimize the risk of failure effective criteria should be set, as with internal development, against which the potential acquisition is judged.

The majority of acquisitions that have taken place in the UK have been horizontal in nature, in that the products acquired have a close relationship with the existing product range, for example the BP acquisition of Alexander Duckhams. A small percentage have been vertical, in that the products involved in the acquisition were previously purchased as raw materials or made from the product manufactured by the acquiring company. ICI's acquisition of various textile companies in order to obtain captive customers falls into this latter category. In the USA, however, the accent has been on lateral acquisition, in that there is no relationship between the products acquired and the existing business. On this basis ITT became a giant conglomerate with such companies as Sheraton Hotels and Avis Car Rentals added to their overall business.

Suppliers

Suppliers of raw materials and packaging are always interested in developing new markets for their own products and frequently come to manufacturers with ideas for new products. An example of this activity is the Metal Box Co, which maintains its own development kitchens looking into possible new canned food recipes. The company publishes a regular bulletin on new products launched into the market and also produces occasional market studies in order to try and stimulate users of cans and bottles to enter various product fields. It is always worthwhile approaching suppliers from time to time on the subject of new products, either through a mailing at periodic intervals or better still through setting up a joint meeting between the supplier and company staff from purchasing, R and D and marketing.

Many ideas obtained in this way may lack potential, but the real danger is that good ideas may be offered by the supplier to more than one customer. After all, his objective is to obtain a high market penetration for his own product. It may be coincidence but occasionally two identical products based on a new ingredient or technological process appear to reach the market simultaneously. For example, in 1966 both Heinz and Crosse and Blackwell launched spaghetti hoop products without either company being aware of the other's interest in the product.

Student projects

It might be possible to obtain the co-operation of university business schools, polytechnics and colleges and involve their students in idea generation. Such educational establishments are often eager to obtain practical exercises for their students which bring contact with industry. Apart from basic intelligence, the student workforce used in this way can present that vital young outlook which ignores traditional taboos. Thus a good brief could lead to really new ideas produced by the generation that will be using tomorrow's products. To illustrate the point, an exercise took place at Iowa University, USA in the 1965–66 academic year in which the students concerned in a project generated over 3,100 new product ideas.

Sponsored research

It might also be possible to sponsor research at a university business school or management college in which the permanent staff of the college research unit undertake market studies, idea generation and even technological development work financed by the company concerned. Crest toothpaste was reputedly developed by a dental student at Columbia University, New York, in research sponsored by Procter and Gamble.

Consultants

Many large companies like to use such outsiders to assist them with their development programme. Birds Eye owe their China Dragon frozen ready meals and RHM Foods their McDougalls Bread Mix to the help of consultants. By using this type of consultancy, often referred to as 'new product workshops', a company can concentrate specialist attention on development without interfering with the on-going management of current products. In addition, a consultant also offers an objective approach not confused by internal company politics.

A consultant could be a separate fee-paid company run by an advertising agency, a division of a management consultancy or an independent marketing consultant. The usual approach of the consultant will be to examine the position of the client company in detail, its objectives, resources and present operation and then set out a plan of action covering markets suitable for investigation. If approved the work will be set in motion to generate ideas.

The advertising agency

The manufacturer's own advertising agency, with or without a specialist new product division, can be a ready-made consultant if given a proper briefing. The agency employs many creative people whose talents can be channelled towards idea generation. But one must not expect too much; as with the manufacturer the agency's main interest tends to lie with its current business. Also it could be difficult for the agency to be truly objective if it stands to gain substantial revenues from the promotion of its own internally-conceived new product. In addition, because the creative expertise within an agency is gained through the promotion of brands, it is probable that the advertising agency comes into its own in cases where the project concerns the development of a new brand in existing markets rather than the identification of an innovative new product. Examples of this include Bryant and May Cooks matches, Trebor Double Agents, KP Outer Spacers and Yardley Laughter fragrance, all of which originated with the help of an advertising agency.

However, innovative product ideas can originate from an agency in the interest of its client. Reputedly, the idea for a new gel hair-setting product, Dippity-Do, came from the president of an advertising agency in the USA. As a hobby he was also a private inventor and the agency went to the extreme of developing and testing the product at its own cost in order to convince a doubting client, the Toni Company.[8]

PRODUCT-ORIENTED TECHNIQUES

Product checklists

The product checklist is simply a series of questions or hypotheses which enables the total view of the product to be expanded. Items considered through the questioning process could include such things as ingredients, flavour, sizes, pack, presentation, price/value relationships, usage, product combinations etc. By bombarding the imagination with queries in this way, ideas in quantity – good, bad and indifferent – can be piled up, leaving judgement to evaluate at a later stage.

There are many questions with which the imagination can be primed such as:[7]

1. Modification: what if this were changed? colour? odour? form (eg liquid, powder, gel)? shape? what other ingredients as alternatives?
2. Addition: what to add? stronger? bigger? longer? thicker? economy size? jumbo? extra ingredient? extra feature?
3. Subtraction: what to subtract? smaller? lighter? condensed? shorter? fewer ingredients? fewer parts? convenience size? pocket size? miniature? what could be eliminated/streamlined?
4. Rearrange: what if features were interchanged? what if this were transposed/combined? another pattern/layout? an assortment? a blend?
5. Usage: who else would like something like this? new ways to use as is/if modified?

The overall objective of the checklist is simply to twist the product around in order to gain a fresh perspective, thus enabling areas of strength and weakness to be assessed. This in turn can lead to new ideas for the product line.

Attribute listing

One checklist approach which follows a set sequence is the technique of attribute listing in which the physical aspects of the product are considered in a systematic manner:

1. Each component of the product is described in factual, physical terms – its shape, dimensions and materials etc.
2. The function of each component is then described – its purpose and the reason for its choice.
3. Each attribute of every component is then considered in turn, changed in all conceivable ways and the changes related to the rest of the product with the objective of discovering some possibility of improvement.

For example,[9] if the attributes of the usual wooden-handled screwdriver were considered, one might list such items as:
1) round, 2) steel shank, 3) wooden handle, riveted thereon, 4) wedge shaped end for engaging slot, 5) manually operated, and 6) torque provided by twisting action. To devise a better screwdriver or even a new

tool perhaps one could focus on each of these attributes separately. The wooden handle could become a plastic handle for longer life and different variations could be thought up with regard to each of the other attributes.

Value analysis

Concentration on the cost of each component in the product attribute list gives us the technique of value analysis. Essentially a cost reduction tool, the technique also can be used imaginatively to redesign existing products and design new ones. Each physical component of the product is assessed to see if it is more expensive than it need be. By examining the cost of providing each component against the function it performs, one can question its worth to the purpose of the whole product and discern areas for simplification, modification or elimination which may then lead to new requirements.

Morphological analysis

Another technique which is concerned with physical attributes is morphological analysis or the heuristic ideation technique, also known as the morphological box. It relies on a detailed examination of the parameters of an existing product type and their rearrangement into different combinations. The first step is to identify the parameters. Whitfield[10] quotes the example of a paint container where the parameters could include size, shape, material, type of closure and colour etc. Each of these is subdivided into every possible form, for example, the parameter 'size' would include ¼ pint, ½ pint, quart, gallon, ½ litre, litre etc. A box or matrix is constructed with each parameter shown as a different dimension. All possible combinations of the subdivisions between parameters are then considered for development. If we follow this simple example of the paint container we would obtain a layout like this:

Size	Shape	Material	Closure
¼ pint	cylindrical	tinplate	press-on lid
½ pint	rectangular	rigid plastic	snap-on lid
1 pint	spherical	flexible plastic	cork
1 quart	conical	paper	shutter
1 gallon	collapsible	glass	spring-loaded stopper
½ litre		aluminium	twist cap
1 litre			

Even with this simple problem 1,260 possible combinations are available for consideration. Not all are practical (a one-gallon, conical, paper container with a twist cap); not all are new (a quart, tinplate, cylindrical container with a press-on lid); but some could offer possibilities for development. Thus morphological analysis gives a multiple view and being largely mechanistic it bypasses personal blind spots, habits and prejudices.

Morphological analysis can be used as the first stage of a systematic three-stage programme. In the first stage[11] the parameters of the product type are established, that is all the conceivable ways in which the product type could be made to vary. Then a decision is made as to which parameters offer possibilities for development. The parameters can be established and the decision made as to which to progress either through personal judgement or with the help of consumer qualitative research.

In the second stage each component of the company's product is described and a decision made, through personal judgement or qualitative research, as to whether the company's product is superior, equal or inferior to competition on each of the components.

Finally, an attempt is made to determine the relative marketing potency of the parameters progressed from stage one and the components evaluated in stage two. Each selected parameter and component is described in a copy capsule, typed on a card (eg 'a hair spray that lasts through thee shampooings') which is presented to consumer groups and rated on a five-point scale. The scale could be based on 'desirability'. In addition, a scale for 'exclusivity' (to your brand alone) and a scale of 'believability' (known and recognized by consumers) can be used.

The end result is a clear picture of strengths and weaknesses of one's own product and the most desirable elements that such a product should possess in the eyes of consumers. The technique can become involved and expensive if consumer research is used at every stage but certainly personal judgement can be used in stages one and two, although the technique may lose a little in potential as a result.

One other technique which appears to have developed from the morphological box concept is that of Scimitar.[12] The technique was developed and used by the New Projects Group of the Steetley Company and later used by the Metal Box Company. Although intended primarily for industrial goods companies, it is perhaps applicable also in the consumer field. The Scimitar model is essentially a three-dimensional matrix (see Figure 6.3) which is constructed to identify gaps in the market rather than new products. The three axes represent the existing raw materials the company uses, the existing processes it applies to those materials and the markets it sells its products in. Blocks are put inside the model to represent all the products the company is already making. So where there is a gap there could be a new product and creative techniques can then be used to help find products to fill the gap.

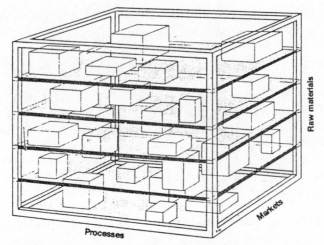

Figure 6.3 The Scimitar three-dimensional matrix

Forced relationships

This technique relies on the creation of an artificial and forced relationship between two or more normally unrelated products or ideas as the starting point for the idea generation process.[13] One example of the method involves consideration of each idea on a list as associated with each other idea on the list. For example, a manufacturer of canned goods could list his products by size and variety and consider each product against each other product on the list. With each consideration the intention would be to stimulate a chain of free associations which might lead to new product ideas.

Letters of complaint

Letters on product performance from consumers and the trade, whether of complaint or praise, might suggest new needs if systematically analysed and thus lead to ideas for products. The idea for the Ford Mustang arose from a consumer letter which then prompted the company to undertake consumer research.

Recipe books and restaurant menu cards

For a food manufacturer, the collection of the above could lead to the identification of popular dishes not yet covered by a branded product, particularly as consumer tastes are gradually becoming more cosmopolitan. Menu cards can be obtained most easily from printers of restaurant menus.

CREATIVITY-ORIENTED TECHNIQUES

Brainstorming

The technique of brainstorming was originated by Alex Osborn in the USA as early as 1938. It can be viewed simply as a creative conference for the sole purpose of producing a checklist of ideas. The name originated because the session entailed using the brain to storm a problem. The technique has become widely used; for example, Heinz Ploughman's Pickle originated in this way. However there is some controversy as to the usefulness of the technique. The term is now defined in the *Concise Oxford Dictionary* as spontaneous discussion in the search for new ideas.

Brainstorming rests on four basic principles:

1. Deferment of judgement – criticism of ideas within the session itself is not allowed, as it is only by suspending judgement that the conventional chains of thought are broken and creativity stimulated, allowing ideas to emerge which would be blocked by the usual critical steps. Evaluation takes place later outside the session.
2. Quantity is the aim, on the basis that the more ideas that result the more likely one is to obtain the best ideas.
3. In pursuit of quantity all ideas are welcome, however wild.
4. Combination and improvement are sought. Mutual stimulation should give rise to ideas, as chance interaction and building on ideas can create a group chain reaction which will produce ideas that none of the participants would otherwise have thought of.

According to Osborn,[7] the ideal group consists of about a dozen people drawn from a mixture of backgrounds, although research conducted by the Battelle Institute[14] indicates that four to seven people may achieve the best results. In order to help break down inhibitions it is important that there should not be differences in status between members and efforts should be made to avoid the formation of cliques. If possible, the members of the group should be recruited on the basis of their creative ability, or at least they should possess above average facility in offering suggestions. A simple test for creativity can be used when recruiting by asking prospective members to give six unusual answers to the question: 'How many uses can you think of for a housebrick?' Ideally the group should have a leader, a deputy leader, five regular members to act as pacesetters and five guests.

A simple and precise brief covering the problem area should be drawn up and sent to the participants two or three days in advance. The brief would be explained in detail by the leader at the beginning of the session and this could be followed by a short warm-up session on a subject, unrelated to the problem in hand. If necessary one or two self-starters can be 'planted' in the group to get the session going. After the warm-up the session itself should last between 20 and 45 minutes. Under the direction of the leader the group are encouraged to roam free mentally, looking beyond obvious solutions and perhaps indulging in a bit of fantasy in their suggestions for new products. Ideas are not identified by the name of the suggestor as this would discourage building on ideas. The one formal aspect of the session is that the ideas should be noted by the leader or deputy leader; the session can also be tape recorded if it is felt that this will not inhibit participants. Any lists of prepared ideas from members should not be allowed but can be handed to the leader beforehand. Once the time period set has expired the session can be closed, or resumed after a short break if it is felt that more ideas are still possible. If required, it might be advantageous to have a change of subject or a different leader. To add greater variety in the second period, word association tests and role playing can be utilized if applicable. Ideally the session should take place in a social context, perhaps in a private room in a hotel, away from the pressures of the office, with refreshments being served. Evaluation should not take place as part of the session and it can take practice to be able to offer less than logical thoughts and to refrain from censuring such thoughts when offered by others.

Time is allowed after the session to enable incubation in the minds of the group members to take place in order to encourage the production of still more ideas to supplement those obtained from the actual session. The leader should contact members by telephone the following day to elicit any further ideas, or this can be done more formally by circulating minutes of the session with space left for additions to be made.

At a later stage the evaluation takes place. This can be done either by a small panel of group members or by outsiders who were not members of the group. Alternatively, as suggested by Rawlinson (1981),[15] all group members may be involved by asking them individually to select their top 10 per cent of ideas from a typed list.

For some sessions it can prove advantageous to set specific guidelines. For example:

1. A typical day: in a search for new toiletry or household products, the group can take as a reference point a typical day from the time a person gets up to the time he or she goes to sleep.
2. Head to toe: this is another set of guidelines in which the body from top to toe and the particular needs of the hair, eyes, mouth, arms etc are considered.
3. In reverse brainstorming the emphasis lies on generating a list of shortcomings concerning a particular product type in order to provide a direction for development discussions.

A modified[16] and more formalized version of the brainstorming technique splits the session into three definite stages lasting for a period of two to four hours. First a discussion takes place on the background information which has been provided. Then the group is divided into subgroups (say nine people into three groups of three) and each subgroup is asked to invent a new product for the market. In the final stage each subgroup presents its product which is evaluated by the other groups.

The members of brainstorming groups are usually recruited from among company employees; for example, members may be senior managers or employees chosen to represent all departments. Alternatively, selection may be confined to specific types of employees, for example salesmen, and also brainstorming can be held among groups of consumers. In order to provide contrast and stimulus, people from a mixture of backgrounds are usually preferable and it is common when groups are formed from within a company to bring in outsiders from, say, the advertising agency or a consultant. It is important that no group must be allowed to feel that it has failed, as guilt feelings can lead to resistance in future groups.

As an extension of brainstorming, the brainwriting methods try to avoid the possible negating effects of group meetings, such as the influence of opinion leaders and dominant personalities. In one method, named the 'brainwriting pool',[14] each of the six to eight participants involved are seated around a table. Each participant puts his ideas on a sheet of paper and in the centre of the table there is already a sheet with some ideas written down before the meeting by the chairman/leader. As soon as one member runs out of ideas he exchanges his sheet with the one in the pool, continuing the list of ideas on the sheet he has received. The task is to consider the ideas on the receiving sheet and to develop them and also hopefully be stimulated by them in the process to develop new ideas. Thus the stimulation to idea generation occurs by written statements without participants being distured or distracted by discussion and they have the opportunity to concentrate on their own thinking during the usual half-hour of a session. However, brainwriting lacks some of the spontaneity of brainstorming's verbal discussions.

Synectics

Known by a name coined from the Greek word meaning the joining together of different and apparently unconnected elements, synectics is a team approach to creative problem solving, drawing together people from a cross-section of the organization. In the qualitative research context the word applies to the integration of diverse individuals with different educational, work and social backgrounds into problem-solving task groups. At its simplest it could be looked on as a form of high-powered brainstorming.

Synectics is based on the belief that the psychological mechanisms that occur in the creative process are usually below the level of consciousness and that the synectics group situation forces each participant to verbalize his thoughts and feelings about the problem in hand. As a result, elements of the creative process can be brought into the open where they can be identified and analysed.

The traditional synectics group comprises five or six individuals of various backgrounds drawn from a single company. The group usually operates with two leaders, one handling administration and the other guiding the actual session. Once the problem is stated, the leader guides the group in a period of free discussion aimed to provide analogies which are relevant to the problem.

The process of free discussion involves two techniques. The first, making the strange familiar, is based on the premise that when the mind is faced with a problem it normally attempts to make the strange familiar by means of analysis, as as strange concept is a threat to security. Thus the mind attempts to force the problem into an acceptable pattern. As a result, making it more familiar through analysis leads to a greater understanding of the problem.

Then the process is reversed to make the familiar strange with the intention of seeing all the implications and possibilities which could lead to a new viewpoint as a basis for the development of a new idea. Synectics has identified four mechanisms for making the familiar strange, each metaphoric in character.

1. Personal analogy: personal identification with the elements of a problem and role playing releases the individual from viewing the problem in terms of its previously analysed elements. For instance the group might consider: 'What would I feel like if I were a closure on this wide-necked bottle?'
2. Direct analogy: considering analogies in nature such as the human mouth or a clam to solve the problem of creating a new type of closure for a bottle. Biology in particular tends to be a rich source of relevant analogies.
3. Symbolic analogy: using recognized images, which might be aesthetically pleasing though technically impossible, to describe the problem, for instance perceiving the closure in terms of the door to Ali Baba's cave.
4. Fantasy analogy: wish fulfilment involving the best of all possible worlds, for instance imagining how in our wildest fantasies we might desire the closure to operate.

Normally fantasy analogy would be used first in this process of conscious self-deceit, as it tends to induce the other analogies. In this way the problem is pushed out of its rigid form and the most pertinent analogies are conceptually compared with the problem to lead to possible new viewpoints which can bring a solution. If inspiration runs dry the sequence can be repeated, perhaps with another leader.

Within a company, synectics can be regarded as an on-going process with the same group meeting weekly for perhaps a day, preferably away from the office, and continuing on a permanent basis or at least for some months. The group should be carefully selected to try and bring together the people with the highest potential creativity. Indeed, as originally devised by Gordon (1981)[17] the group, meeting on a full-time basis, can often work as an independent entity within the company and is chosen after a rigorous selection procedure and trained over a long period of time.

Sessions to meet specific needs are more likely to be run by outside consultants on an *ad hoc* basis. The synectics formalized approach is adopted in sessions which aim for a solution in around 45 to 60 minutes. The group consists of a leader, a client and about five participants, and there are eight specific stages. In the first two the problem and the background to it are stated by the client. Then the participants restate the problem in a series of 'How to . . . ' statements from which the client selects those to be progressed. The ideas are developed in a mental excursion using metaphors and analogies in stages 5 and 6 when participants are encouraged to fantasize toward a solution and then 'force-fit' these fantasies in stage 7 to the reality of the problem. In the final stage the client commits himself to a possible solution or 'viewpoint'. The process may be repeated if necessary until a satisfactory solution is found. Prince[18] gives examples of the problems dealt with at such sessions, which range from ideas for new tooth cleaning products for children to the disposal of garbage from Polaris submarines.

Lateral thinking

Lateral thinking is the alternative to vertical thinking as the way of arriving at ideas. Vertical thinking is careful logical analysis. It depends on taking the most reasonable view of a situation and proceeding logically and carefully to work out an answer. This is the way we all naturally tend to think – in a straightforward manner. Vertical thinking is straight ahead thinking which can give rise to the most probable effective action; it assumes that an existing situation is a useful stepping stone to something better. But it can be inhibiting sometimes to the birth of new ideas, as it requires as a starting point a basic accepted structure representing the current situation. The mind provides an environment for incoming information to organize itself into patterns. The sequence in which information arrives determines the patterns that form and as a result new ideas tend to be based on existing patterns. Thus vertical thinking often leads to alterations in accepted ideas rather than new ideas, to product modification rather than new products.

With lateral thinking, a term coined by de Bono (1967),[19] the mind tends to arrive at ideas through exploring various ways of looking at things, consequently restructuring existing patterns of information in the mind. While the vertical thinker continues down the same path, the lateral thinker moves sideways, trying different paths until the right one is selected and a new idea is born. Lateral thinking sets out to avoid the logical progression of thought from the status quo by emphasizing different ways of viewing a situation. As a result it can remain free from the well-tried familiar patterns on which vertical thinking depends.

This search for alternative ways of looking at things is not natural. The natural tendency of the mind is to become impressed by current ideas and proceed from there. To overcome this and to start thinking laterally it is necessary to be deliberate. This involves two basic processes:

1. Escape: recognition of a dominant or polarizing idea, self-imposed boundaries and unchallenged assumptions.
2. Provocation: making unjustified leaps in thought, the use of chance, movement for the sake of movement, in order to generate a new direction.

One technique involving these two processes is to turn things upside down by reversing a relationship. For instance, a manufacturer of wall coverings could start in his search for ideas from the concept of the wall being suspended from the ceiling rather than as a support for the ceiling.

Another technique is to think in terms of visual images. The physical act of shaving as imagined in visual terms could well have highlighted the inconvenience of changing blades and led to wind-on cassette, cartridge and blade injector razors.

A further technique is to predetermine the number of ways in which a situation can be looked at. A new drink could be not only a thirst quencher but a supply of vitamins, a source of taste and flavour, a diet food, an energy source, a replenishment of lost body salts, a geriatric food, a children's food, an instant meal, a body builder and others.

Shifting emphasis from one part of a problem to another is a further technique. In considering convenience foods one could start at the housewife's impression of a product in a pan on the cooker rather than the family's impression of the product on a plate.

Creating a problem which does not yet exist is another good starting point for lateral thinking. The assumption that the uniformity in taste of cigarettes could be a problem could lead to cigarette holders that add different flavours to the taste. Similarly, distortion of a situation can help, for example the belief that people have too tiny a stomach could lead to new foods that foam up from a small amount to a large but light and fluffy portion.

Also basic to lateral thinking is the use of chance in the generation of new ideas. Without interfering with the chance process it is possible to provide a suitable setting in which it may operate. Chance may be employed through exposing oneself to stimulants by wandering around some place that is full of things which one would not deliberately seek out, a junk yard being one example. Also visits to a store or to an exhibition in which nothing is specifically looked for, but where the visitor is ready to consider anything that attracts the attention, could be of value. Products seen on a shelf can lead to ideas for products in completely different markets. The idea for the sweet sauces for puddings marketed by HP and Walls possibly could have arisen from a chance contemplation of the ketchup and brown sauce shelf facings in a store.

Lateral thinking is basically an individual matter, although it also plays a part in several group situations, such as brainstorming and synectics. It is a way of using information to bring about creativity in a deliberate way. This need arises from the nature of the mind as a self-organizing information system which establishes fixed patterns. Lateral thinking can restructure these patterns, escaping from old ideas to bring about new ones. But it is not usually a substitute for vertical thinking; the two are complementary. Lateral thinking can identify a new idea but vertical thinking may then be necessary to develop it, and when vertical thinking can do no more then lateral thinking can change the approach so that vertical thinking can proceed again. Sometimes lateral thinking can provide a solution by itself, but more often it needs to be in combination with vertical thinking to provide an approach to idea generation.

CONSUMER-ORIENTED TECHNIQUES

Group discussions

Consumer group discussions can generate ideas when face-to-face interviews, with an interviewer waiting for a reply, will not. Being qualitative and discursive, the research can be fairly comprehensive and exhaustive without running into difficulties with questionnaire design and interview fatigue. In this way unsatisfied needs and aspirations can be consciously looked for. Once found these needs can become the new starting point for a deliberate attempt at new concept formulation. For example, group discussions among housewives revealed the guilt feelings that were present around shop-bought cakes. This led to the Mr Kipling image embracing warm, semi-Victorian packs and an attempt to get the home-made look to products on the bakery line.

Discussion in the group takes place within a loose framework and the interaction that occurs between members can produce ideas that would not arise from a single interview. The discussion enables respondents to warm up gradually, lose their inhibitions and to stop answering questions in too well thought out and rational a way. The group, consisting of six to 12 people, are guided by a leader (often skilled in psychology) who takes them from familiar areas (eg the use of children's toys) to more speculative areas (suggestions for new toys). The discussion often starts with expressed satisfactions and dissatisfactions with existing products as the members go through present behaviour and usage patterns in order to identify specific problems.

This process can be extended into role playing by reconstructing a given set of activities. For example, the domestic hot plate could have been suggested by determining in a group how a woman can serve a meal in a servantless house, trying simultaneously to be a gracious hostess, keeping all food hot and eliminating many of the kinds of accidents that occur in passing food. By reconstructing actual or imaginary behaviour the leader/psychologist may be able to pinpoint a trouble spot which can then become the core of a product concept, whereas if he was to ask the group directly to articulate a need, the result would very likely be a complete blank.

As a technique, group discussions are mainly criticized on the grounds that the group members find it difficult to hypothesize and direct their thinking from existing products, resulting in ideas for line extenders rather than for wholly new products. There is probably some truth in this criticism and real problem-solving ability on the part of the leader/psychologist is often required in order to close the gap between expressed needs and the possible product solution.

Consumer panels

A variant on the group discussion is the dissatisfaction panel or focus group,[20] consisting of a group of consumers who are literally paid to grumble about existing products. The intention is that by exposing the problems in relation to existing products then new product ideas may arise.

In problem inventory analysis[21] the group are presented with a list of problems (devised by the development team as relevant) and asked, for each, which products come to mind as having the problem. This procedure can be followed where it is felt that in a specific product category, it is easier for consumers to relate products to problems rather than generate problems for a given product.

Pseudo product tests

Pseudo product tests can often be used in groups and can form the framework for the discussion.[22] An existing product in a pack which is flashed 'new formula' or 'new improved' or some other point of differentiation is compared with an identical product in its normal packaging. The way in which people think the product is improved can be a guide to the way in which they would like it improved. So strong can be the power of suggestion that often identical products can be sampled and the majority of the group will identify a perceived difference. The author conducted such a test among a group with two identical bottles of tomato ketchup, except that one was labelled 'with apple and added vitamins'. The group overwhelmingly preferred the taste of the latter product.

Depth interviews

The problem areas revealed by a group can often be pursued further through depth interviews among selected members of the group or among new people entirely. Indeed, depth interviews can be used instead of a group discussion particularly in those product fields where it is felt that much of the motivation for purchase may lie at an unconscious level.

Activity analysis

One form of qualitative research than can be used is activity analysis,[23] also known as functional analysis and the action study. Such studies take the form of a very detailed analysis of consumer behaviour in an area of interest to the manufacturer. They attempt to answer the question: 'What kind of work is performed by the consumer and how can I help her to simplify her work and make it easier?' For instance, a housewife might agree to a researcher spending a day with her in the kitchen and about the home, watching her at work, regarding what she does and why she does it, assessing her likes and dislikes about each task and the products she uses to help her. From a number of such studies the areas of market opportunity can be assessed and creative minds then put to work to devise product concepts to meet the consumer need.

An alternative approach to the researcher in the home is to film a working day. The films can then be exhaustively sifted to draw conclusions about possible needs and can be used as recall aids when informants are subsequently interviewed in depth about their feelings and frustrations at each point in the 'action'.

Activity analysis is particularly applicable to sourcing ideas for labour-saving products of the 'disposable, single application, self-cleaning' type of concepts as well as for small domestic appliances. They can also be useful for more everyday products, when the technique is adapted to the diary method. For example, a panel of women might keep a record of their use of toiletry and cosmetic products over a short period of time as a detailed diary of 'action' data.

Past consumer research

Reading previous research reports, both qualitative and quantitative, very comprehensively and with a detailed eye in a focused attempt to discern new product openings, is a simple and straightforward search method. Such reports could embrace usage and attitude studies, product tests, advertisement tests and group discussions etc. Ideas might come, for instance, from the open-ended like and dislike questions about existing brands or from the revelation that one of them has a subsidiary use. Research reports can also be examined on a segmentation basis, first of all by product type, for instance, to see if there are opportunities for a gel instead of a cream and second by consumer groups, for example to see if there is a large enough group to justify a premium product.

It can also be valuable to ensure that all possible 'new product inventors' within a company, particularly R and D personnel, are exposed to this data, although a new product manager sitting down to read all the consumer research in the company archives, with his eye deliberately open for opportunities, might think of the idea which could elude others who were reading more spasmodically.

COMPETITION-ORIENTED TECHNIQUES

The 'me too' approach

The basis of this approach, which is attributed to the A C Nielsen Co Ltd, is that an opportunity may sometimes be identified if one looks for a market where one brand heavily dominates with a 70 per cent or more brand share. This may allow entry to the market if a viable product difference can be established. Some years ago Heinz entered the canned custard market then dominated by Ambrosia with a product with a viable difference. Heinz installed an aseptic canning line, a process which resulted in a product with a longer shelf life and consequently leadership in the market eventually fell to Heinz.

The 'me too' approach need not necessarily be confined to markets dominated by a single brand. Studying the attributes of one's product in relation to all competitive products may reveal omissions in the product category which can be exploited. Several years ago Lever Brothers looked at floor cleaning products and came up with Dual, a product which both cleaned and polished.

Simply copying a competitive product is also a variation on the 'me too' approach. One looks for a market that appears to be growing and which can support more than the present number of brands in the market. Brooke Bond with Brazilian Blend coffee, Reckitts with Cleen-o-Pine cream cleanser and Birds Eye with frozen pancakes took this path. Indeed, the result of a study undertaken by Cooper (1979)[24] suggested that the advantages to a manufacturer of being 'first in' to a market was almost as equally balanced by as many pitfalls and disadvantages.

Studying competitors' products and trade magazines, perhaps supported by salesmen's reports and market data, will help discover markets where a 'me too' approach can be adopted.

Trade opinion surveys

It is also possible to consult the trade, although the ideas that result are likely to be variants of products already on the market. Surveys and/or group discussions among trade buyers and store managers should indicate what types of new product the trade thinks are likely to sell. This should at least ensure some measure of distribution for the suggested new product once it is developed. The marketing consultants Kraushar, Andrews and Eassie Ltd have undertaken on occasions a survey to obtain ideas on the product fields where development opportunities exist, in the opinion of the trade buyers concerned.

Market analysis

The whole process of analysing market data that takes place in the planning stage can often lead directly to ideas. Such a study led to the launch of Rowntree's Yorkie bar. The market data include trends, competition, product life cycles and behavioural data etc. It is more than likely that the opportunities revealed will entail copying a competitor although innovative ideas can occur sometimes in a creative manner.

Store visits

Ideas can also occur from simple store visits and it can be valuable to organize these on a regular basis. Store visits have been mentioned in relation to overseas markets and as part of the lateral thinking process. However, a detailed study of products on shelves in domestic markets where one is consciously looking in a systematic way for new ideas can sometimes be rewarding. The opportunity may arise to copy a competitor in a possible growth market, pinpoint a neglected market segment or introduce a new line based on an existing concept.

OTHER SPECIALIZED TECHNIQUES

Segmentation analysis

The concept of market segmentation introduced by Smith (1956)[25] refers to the notion that a market for a product is composed of subgroups, each of which has different needs or wants and each of which, therefore, possesses a homogenous purchase behaviour. The subgroup can be identified by one or more 'people' characteristics. By clustering the market into groups it may be possible to identify a significant segment who appear to have a latent, unsatisfied need which can give rise to a new product opportunity. The concept is illustrated by the introduction of Horizon Holidays, which were aimed at a middle-class segment at a time when all packaged tour operators targeted the mass market.

The data relevant to the 'people' characteristics which can be collected in order to identify groups include:

1. Demographic data: age, sex, socio-economic group, income levels, geographical regions etc.
2. Social structure: social class, norms of behaviour, style of living, reference group influences, social aspirations etc.
3. Personality variables: common personality traits such as aggression and the desire to dominate etc.

The non-demographic characteristics were emphasized by Yankelovich[26] who extended the range of people characteristics to include:

4. Usage patterns: analysis of the various uses a product is put to in order to pinpoint particular uses which a new product might satisfy better.
5. Attitudinal factors: price/value relationships, purchase motivation, aesthetic preference etc.

Research techniques which can be used to identify subgroups on the basis of the two latter groups of characteristics include usage and attitude surveys, concept tests, group discussions and depth interviews etc. The information may be available from all the previous research data the company has collected, or specially devised research can be set up in which the relevant data is collected from a large sample of the market. Once the survey is completed the market is then clustered into groups in terms of the data and depth interviews carried out, to try and discover if there are groups who appear to have latent, unsatisfied needs.

Another method, relevant only to attitudinal factors, would be to identify these factors from depth interviews/group discussions and then carry out a quantitative survey in which consumers are asked to rate ideal brands according to the list of identified attributes. Factor or cluster analysis could then be used to split consumers into groups with similar sets of attitudes in order to establish if a large subgroup exists with a common set of attitudes to a product.

Many new products have been developed on the basis of 'people' characteristics. These would include, for example, some of the products aimed at the young person's market (drinks, fashion goods etc). But segmentation by people characteristics tends to be a little insensitive, in that the subgroups can be too broad to reveal product opportunities. Also a product often appeals across several subgroups, making it difficult to discern one group with a homogenous purchase behaviour distinct from other groups. The technique perhaps is of most value in revealing market potential, for example the quantification of older age groups in relation to geriatric products.

The above approach to market segmentation rests on identifying differences among people who comprise markets. Another approach which concentrates on differences among products in a market was first outlined by Kuehn and Day[27] in 1962. The basis of the method is that people differentiate between brands according to their perception of the brand's characteristics and then choose the brand whose characteristics they prefer. It is suggested, for example, that consumer preference for a product such as chocolate cake mix is normally distributed along some key dimension, in this case 'chocolateyness'. The majority of consumers will prefer a satisfactory level of the key ingredient, that is a 'chocolatey' cake mix. As a result the tendency is for all manufacturers to introduce products which are similar, as they are built around the majority preference for the same level of 'chocolateyness'. However, there might be large minorities for whom the new product could be devised, who prefer a stronger or weaker level of 'chocolateyness', which overall product preference tests would fail to allow for. To discover if a large minority exists it would be necessary to conduct a preference test (see Figure 6.4) in which consumers place their preference for the significant characteristic on a product attitude scale. In practice, there may be more than one significant characteristic and preference tests would have to be conducted for each major characteristic.

A second approach[28] to segmentation by product seeks to establish subgroups through revealing consumer ideas about similarities between brands. The method, known as market structure analysis, utilizes a pattern of research techniques in which:

1. Group discussions are held to determine which brands are seen as competing for the same uses and the characteristics that make these brands similar.

2. With this information it is then possible to hypothesize new combinations of these characteristics, perhaps including other feasible new characteristics, thereby identifying new opportunities.
3. This is followed by a small-scale preference study to establish the proportion of consumers who like both the current brands and the proposed new brands.
4. Finally, a large-scale preference study is held to discover the proportion of consumers who would prefer each new product to their current brand.

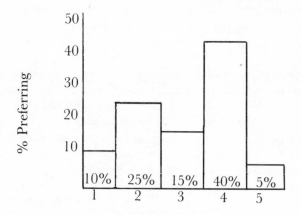

Figure 6.4 *Distribution of preference between different levels of 'chocolateyness'*

In traditional market segmentation the identification of subgroups is based on the characteristics of the consumer, whereas in segmentation by product the criteria used are the characteristics of the product. Both forms of segmentation are likely to result in the design of products that fill in the product line as extensions of existing products rather than completely new innovations. Common to both methods is the principle that the needs of consumers in relation to a product group can vary and as a result companies can be successful through catering for the smaller groups. However, the smaller group should be large enough to make the introduction of a product worthwhile. The market for hair shampoo in the USA illustrates that the distance between successful segmentation and wasteful fragmentation can be short. Here, segmentation by product type (cream, gel, concentrate, liquid, lotion), hair type (oily, dry, normal), hair colour (blonde, brunette, redhead, grey) and container (plastic, glass, tube, aeorsol) led to such a bewildering array of products that many could not hope to gain a satisfactory sales volume.

Technological forecasting

The techniques which are included under the general title of technological forecasting are concerned, as the name implies, with predicting future technologies and their implications. The forecaster cannot predict the precise nature and form of the technology which will dominate a given application at some specific future date, but he can use the techniques to enhance his judgement and make 'range forecasts' of the performance characteristics a particular class of technology will be able to provide at some future point in time. He can also analyse the implications and assess the opportunities that may arise for the company as a result.

Thus technological forecasting is concerned with evaluating the significance of various possible future developments so that managers can make better long-term corporate planning decisions. It is not concerned directly with the generation of ideas for new products which may result from technological change, although the results of the forecasting can give a better idea of future development possibilities and direct R and D along a more effective route. But as a by-product, ideas for new products can arise in a creative manner by virtue of utilizing the techniques and analysing their results.

It is not the place here to make a detailed study of the techniques available, as technological forecasting is not normally the responsibility of the new products manager. In addition, the subject has been covered in detail elsewhere.[29] Although having relevance to most consumer markets, it is perhaps more directly applicable to the industrial goods field. But the techniques require some coverage, in order that their secondary value as a source of ideas may be more easily appreciated.

A variety of techniques have been developed and, as with all other forecasting methods, the most effective are based on an analysis of past experience combined with the insight of imaginative and competent people. The various methods are best used in combination in order to stimulate more creative analysis.

Perhaps the most well known technique is the Delphi model, developed by the Rand Corporation in the USA. A group of experts, representing allied technologies, are asked individually (or in a number of subgroups) to predict the timing and the implication of advances in a technology as it is developed towards its ultimate potential. Discussion, with its tendency to distort through pressure from seniority and from the majority opinion, is eliminated. Without allowing face-to-face confrontation between the experts, controlled feedback takes place, identifying areas where there are reasonable agreements or disagreements and then a second opinion is asked for. This can be repeated until an acceptable degree of consensus is reached, which can then be used as a basis for calculating probability

THE GENERATION OF IDEAS FOR NEW PRODUCTS

statements in a consolidated forecast.

Similar in objective if not in method is the 'theoretical limits test', in which forecasters deliberately push a technological application to the furthest limits in theory to which it can be extended. An attempt is then made to visualize its potential application.

On the other hand, with 'normative relevance trees' the forecaster works backwards from the future rather than forwards. An objective is determind (eg the need for new forms of heat and light by the year 2000 AD) and the alternative routes by which it can be achieved are thoroughly evaluated.

Thus, with the latter two methods a systems approach is adopted which embraces:

1. The impact study: analysing the technical, economic and social implications of possible new technological solutions, that is attempting to answer the question, 'if a technology could achieve the following capacities what would be the results?'
2. Posing hypothetical future problems and then defining the characteristics of technologies needed to solve them.

The technique of 'demand assessment' is based on the belief that demand tends to be the primary force in stimulating technological change. It seeks to identify future needs on the basis of historical and present trends, needs which would be inadequately met by current technologies. It can be viewed as an extension to normal market research methods.

Technological forecasting must ultimately predict whether technical systems can reach or exceed key levels or parameters of performance by certain future dates. The technique of 'parameter analysis' centres on selecting and predicting these parameters. Certain methods have been developed for this purpose:

1. Predicting technological changeover points through defining the critical performance characteristics which will enable one technology to substitute for another.
2. Analysing substitution growth curves to help show how rapidly one technology will actually take over from another. Historical cases where substitution has already begun can be used and applied to new situations.
3. Analysing the unique properties of a product in a similar way to morphological analysis, but to identify where a product can be most readily substituted for other products.

Useful forecasts about the future nature and implications of existing early stage research can often be made through scientific surveys. A review is made of all the existing research in a field, using an internal staff group and/or advisory committee of outside specialists. Such research is based on past experience and depends on these past patterns continuing into the future, but it can help predict future development and the problems that research is likely to solve in the foreseeable future.

Certain forecasting techniques are concerned with predicting how competitors' technical actions will affect the company. Monitoring publications, annual reports, patents, merger activity, acquisitions and new product introductions can form the basis of several approaches such as:

1. Life cycle models plotting product life cycles to help predict the form and degree of future product substitutions and thus help direct R and D activity to effective channels.
2. Technological mapping: competitors' technological strengths in various fields of interest are evaluated by network techniques in order to assist the company to seek out technical approaches which are attractive and avoid those in which competition is likely to be dominant.
3. Strategic analysis: involves monitoring and evaluating acquisitions, new product introductions etc to indicate where competitors will place their technological emphasis. As a result the company can marshal its own resources where its relative strengths are greatest.

Technological forecasting is still a new field and many believe that it is an art relying on human judgement, rather than a science relying on factual data. Despite its limitations it can help improve decisions in the area of corporate planning by giving a clearer delineation of future technological opportunities and threats to the company. The limitations that arise are concerned with the possibility of inadequate source data and the inability of the various techniques to predict totally unexpected breakthroughs. The limitations may be a weakness in the corporate planning context, but they are of little consequence to the actual quantity and quality of new product ideas that may be generated as a by-product of the technological forecasting process.

REFERENCES

1 Frost W and Braine R, 'The application of the repertory grid techniques to problems in market research', *Commentary*, July 1967.
2 Clemens J and Thornton C, 'Evaluating non-existent products', *Admap*, Vol 4, No 5, May 1968.
3 Douglas G, Kemp P and Cook J, *Systematic New Product Development*, Gower, 1983.
4 Roberts E D, 'What do we really know about managing R and D', *Research Management*, November 1978.
5 Greenhalgh C, 'Generating new product ideas', *Admap*, September, October, November 1971.

6 Sowrey J T, *Idea Generation: The Sourcing of Ideas for New Products in Consumer Markets,* Doctoral thesis, University of Strathclyde, 1984.

7 Osborn A F, *Applied Imagination,* Charles Scribners' Sons, 1957.

8 Gerlach J T and Wainwright C A, *Successful Management of New Products,* Hastings House, 1968.

9 McPherson J H, 'The people, the problems and the problem solving methods', *Guide to Creative Action* (Parnes S J *et al*), Charles Scribners' Sons, 1977.

10 Whitfield P R, *Creativity in Industry,* Penguin Books, 1975.

11 Twedt D W, 'How to plan new products, improve old ones and create better advertising', *Journal of Marketing,* January 1969.

12 Carson J W and Rickards T, *Industrial New Product Development,* Gower, 1979.

13 Souder W E and Ziegler R W, 'A review of creativity and problem solving techniques', *Research Management,* Vol 20, No 4, 1977.

14 Schlicksupp H, 'Idea generation for industrial firms – report on an international investigation', *R and D Management,* Vol 2, No 7, 1977.

15 Rawlinson J C, *Creative Thinking and Brainstorming,* Gower, 1981.

16 Sampson P, 'Can consumers create new products', *Market Research Society Journal,* Vol 12, Pt 1, January 1970.

17 Gordon W J J, *Synectics, the Development of Creative Capacity,* Harper and Row, 1961.

18 Prince G M, *The Practice of Creativity,* Harper and Row, 1970.

19 de Bono, E, *The Use of Lateral Thinking,* Jonathan Cape, 1967.

20 Fern E F, 'The use of Focus Groups for idea generation', *Journal of Marketing Research,* February, 1982.

21 Tauber E M, 'Discovering new product opportunities with problem inventory analysis', *Journal of Marketing,* January 1975.

22 King S H M, 'Identifying market opportunities', *Management Decision,* Vol 9, Pt 1, 1971.

23 White R, *Consumer Product Development,* Longman, 1973.

24 Cooper R G, 'The dimensions of industrial new product success and failure', *Journal of Marketing,* Vol 43, Summer 1979.

25 Smith W, 'Product differentiation and market segmentation as alternative marketing strategies', *Journal of Marketing,* July 1956.

26 Yankelovich D, 'New criteria for market segmentation', *New Product Development* (ed Eastlack J O Jnr), American Marketing Association, 1968.

27 Kuehn A A and Day R L, 'Strategy of product quality', *Harvard Business Review,* Nov/Dec 1962.

28 Barnett M K, 'Beyond market segmentation', *Harvard Business Review,* Vol 43, Jan/Feb 1968.

29 Quinn J B, 'Technological forecasting', *Harvard Business Review,* March/April 1967.

Chapter 7 Identifying the most useful techniques

INTRODUCTION

There appear to have been very few research studies that have attempted to evaluate the various sources and techniques and identify those that could be the most useful to companies in generating ideas for new products. A limited number of studies have attempted to evaluate a particular technique, for example Parnes (1961)[1] and Bouchard (1972)[2] with brainstorming. But the author, after a comprehensive search, was able to identify only four studies in the UK that could be used to indicate the most useful techniques from a wide range.

STUDY 1

A survey was conducted by Greenhalgh (1971),[3] using Shaw's 'Price List' as a source list, to identify manufacturers who had launched a grocery brand into the UK market in 1970. Marketing directors of these companies were asked two basic questions by means of a postal survey: first, to specify where the idea for the product came from and second, to classify the product as a success or a failure. The survey obtained 121 effective replies representing a response rate of 22 per cent.

As a result of the survey Greenhalgh identified three generic sources which accounted for the majority of replies:

		%
1.	Market searching (including accidental 'one-offs')	40
2.	Consumer research (including past research)	24
3.	Research and development	14
		78

Within these broad categories there were four techniques among the 26 listed which appeared to be the most important for their ability to generate new product ideas, although the success or failure of the product resulting from the idea is not taken into consideration at this stage. The four most important techniques were:

1. Identification of growth areas by market study.
2. Following competition (including associated companies) after search of UK markets.
3. A by-product from previous consumer research.
4. A scientific/technical/R and D breakthrough.

When only those products were considered which the marketing directors anticipated would be a success then the following expanded range of techniques was identified as important:

	Anticipated product successes %
Identification of a growth area by market study	17
Following competitors (including associated companies) after search of UK markets	12
Following/anticipating competition after noticing their movements	8
Branding a commodity	8
A scientific/technical/R and D breakthrough	7
A by-product from previous consumer research	7
An organized search of foreign markets	7
A one-off suggestion from a foreign market (including parent company or subsidiaries)	6
Creative flair/'out-of-the-blue'	6

Thus the four techniques which generated the most ideas were also important for their ability to generate ideas for successful products (according to the performance of the product at the time of the survey).

The study also examined sources of ideas by type of product, categorizing grocery products into nine groups. These were savoury foods, sweet foods, snack foods, beverages, other food/drink, animal products, household products, toiletries/medicines and smoking products. Although the small number of products in some of the categories inhibits the validity of generalizations, there do not appear to be any dramatic differences between product groups. The main divergences from the general pattern were the importance of R and D for savoury foods and the preponderance of market research based products in the household category and of consumer research based brands among the smoking products, the latter at the expense of R and D.

It should be emphasized that the Greenhalgh survey was confined to products sold through UK grocery outlets. Also, the question used in relation to idea generation was multiple choice and offered a list of 26 possible sources. This could have brought some bias to the replies by confining them to the predetermined pattern established by the list. In addition, because the survey included products in test market, respondents were asked to predict whether the product was likely to be a success or a failure. In some cases such a prediction would inevitably produce a positive answer that had a subjective bias towards success.

STUDY 2

Mandry (1973)[4] also conducted a study into new product development in the UK grocery trade. The study embraced many aspects of development and it included an identification of techniques used by companies to generate ideas for new products. In scope it covered branded food and drink products sold through the UK grocery trade. It excluded semi-commodity type products such as bread, fresh meats, fish, eggs, fresh fruit, vegetables and milk. Alcohol, ice cream and confectionery were also excluded. The study was confined to companies over £5 million in turnover and consisted of 35 units, a unit being defined as either the whole company or a division of a company.

The information was collected in 1971 through a combination of personal interview and self-completion questionnaire. However, there was a high refusal rate and only 15 units agreed to complete all or part of the questionnaire. The remainder refused on the grounds of time or confidentiality. Thus it cannot be claimed that the sample was in any way representative of all the major food companies operating in the UK grocery market.

The sources of ideas for new products varied. Most companies carried out scanning of overseas markets on an organized basis, although the level of sophistication in this respect varied. Some companies carried out in-depth studies which included a physical analysis of all new products in market areas of interest, but to other companies market scanning meant a visit to the USA every couple of years. Five of the companies claimed to have made use of an advertising agency, three used brainstorming and two had made use of synectics. Gap analysis techniques aroused mixed feelings. Two companies were intending to launch brands developed out of gap analysis but a number were extremely sceptical about the technique.

STUDY 3

A study of new product development was conducted by Randall (1980)[5] on behalf of the British Institute of Management. A postal survey was carried out in 1978, embracing 975 companies who were members of the BIM. A total of 330 companies returned the questionnaire and these were of varying size, representing a cross-section of manufacturing industries in the UK. They included both consumer and industrial companies as the sample was selected by random sampling techniques from the 17 categories defined by the Standard Industrial Classification.

The study was primarily concerned with how companies organized themselves for new product development, but the survey identified a total of 11 sources of ideas for new products. These are listed below in order of importance, that is in an order determined by the frequency of usage by companies:

1. Technical knowledge within the company.
2. Bright ideas within the company.
3. Sales office suggestions.
4. Competitive activities.
5. Customer suggestions.
6. Problems from customer operations.
7. Other internal research.
8. Suppliers' innovations.
9. Arising from problems in the company's operation.
10. Academic research.
11. Market research/market requirements.

Since the survey did not attempt to identify successful new products it is not possible to relate the techniques to product performance. Most ideas originated from within the company, while the most used outside sources involved competition and customers.

STUDY 4

A comprehensive study of sources and techniques used to generate ideas for new products was undertaken by the author (Sowrey, 1984).[6] The study was concerned with consumer products and embraced both fast-moving consumer goods and consumer durables. The prime objectives of the study were:

1. To determine whether companies who utilized a considerable number of techniques were more likely to develop successful new products than those who did not.
2. To establish which methods were used to practice.
3. To identify which of the methods used by companies were likely to be of the most value.
4. To discover whether creative methods were more fruitful in producing good ideas than those which were analytical, or whether the opposite was the case. (The term 'good ideas' was used in the sense of quality rather than volume.)

5. To test the hypothesis that companies tend to emphasize the use of analytical methods and neglect those that are creative in character.

The survey work took place in three stages. First, a personal interview survey in 1977 with 10 well-known national companies, the purpose of which was to provide the necessary framework to facilitate the design of a questionnaire. This was then followed by the main postal survey which was completed in 1978 and embraced 245 companies, selected by random sampling methods from a source list based on *The Times'* 1,000 largest UK companies and their subsidiaries. The survey produced a 39 per cent response rate, that is 95 companies completed questionnaires. A qualitative in-depth study within two companies in 1981–82 formed the third stage. This final stage was concerned with providing overt behavioural data in order to enable a better understanding of the development process, particularly idea generation, to be obtained.

In relation to the research objectives, the findings indicated that there did appear to be a strong relationship between the number of techniques used by a company and the number of successful products developed by that company. The greater the number of techniques used, the greater the number of successful products developed; the fewer the number of techniques used, the fewer the number of products.

Number of techniques used	Number of companies	Average number of successful products
40 and over	3	3.0
30 to 39	13	2.8
20 to 29	36	2.2
20 to 10	33	1.8
9 and less	10	0.5

However, it should be stated that a definite causal link was not established, as in theory other variables might possibly have played a part in producing the relationship. But in practice it would appear reasonable to assume that the number of techniques used has a causal relationship with the number of successful products developed.

In relation to the second research objective, a list of 66 sources and techniques was included in the postal questionnaire; these were discussed in detail in Chapter 6. A reasonable proportion of these, at 38, were in widespread use, in that they were used by 20 per cent of the sample. Techniques that were described in the questionnaire as competition-oriented and also those that looked to overseas markets were the most widely used. Two techniques in particular were used by a high proportion of companies: examining competitor's products (83 per cent) and store visits (81 per cent), both of which were classified as competition-oriented. There were 10 techniques which were used by over 60 per cent of companies. In order of popularity these were:

1. Competitors' products.
2. Store visits.
3. Overseas store visits.
4. Market analysis.
5. Overseas trade magazines.
6. Overseas sister company.
7. Overseas exhibitions.
8. Trade magazines.
9. R and D department.
10. Consumer group discussions.

Although many techniques were used both by companies selling fast-moving consumer goods and those selling consumer durables, there were also a large number which were used extensively by only companies in one of these product groups. For example, the advertising agency was used by 66 per cent of fast-moving consumer goods companies but only 24 per cent of consumer durables companies, and consumer complaints analysis was used by 56 per cent of the latter but only 20 per cent of the former.

However, the techniques used within companies were not necessarily the ones which produced ideas for successful products. In order to determine the techniques which had proved to be of most value, the respondents were asked if they had launched a successful new product in the last two years and where the idea for that product came from. On this basis 16 main sources were identified. Some of the sources described by respondents were broad in nature and might encompass a number of separate techniques. For example, consumer research as a quoted source could embrace group discussions, depth interviews, attitude surveys etc. Bearing this in mind, by far the most productive source was the marketing department, followed by R and D, consumer research and market analysis.

Source quoted by companies	Number of successful products
Marketing department	38
R and D department	15
Consumer research	13
Market analysis	12
Advertising agency	10
Competition	9
Overseas	9
Segmentation analysis	8

Salesforce	6
Overseas sister company	6
Supplier	5
Outside inventor	2
Licensing	2
Outside consultant	1
Brainstorming	1
Gap analysis	1

In addition, respondents were asked to rate each source and technique in the list of 66 on the questionnaire on a scale from 1 (highest) to 4 (lowest), according to how they regarded each technique with respect to its value in generating ideas for successful new products. On this basis, the techniques below were rated the most highly and are arranged in order of merit.

Techniques	Average rating	Number of companies responding
Market analysis	1.6	62
Consumer group discussions	1.6	50
Consumer depth interviews	1.7	37
Pseudo product tests	1.7	19
Competitors' products	1.8	75
Marketing think tank	1.8	42
R and D department	1.9	52
Licensing/joint venture	1.9	39
Outside consultant	1.9	39
Overseas sister company	2.0	58
Segmentation analysis	2.0	22

As a result of their value in practice in generating ideas for successful new products, and on the basis of the rating awarded by companies as to their perceived value, it is possible to suggest which would be the top 10 techniques or sources likely to be the most productive in generating ideas for successful new products. These are arranged below in order of merit:

1. Marketing think tank.
2. Market analysis.
3. Consumer group discussions.
4. Consumer depth interviews.
5. R and D department.
6. Competitors' products.
7. Overseas sister company.
8. Advertising agency.

9. Segmentation analysis.
10. A supplier.

The evidence with regard to the value of creative techniques as compared with analytical techniques was more difficult to assess. The two types of technique are difficult to compare because of the problems involved in defining just what is a creative technique as opposed to one which is analytical. For the purpose of the research, creative techniques were defined as those which laid emphasis on creating a situation which stimulated the imagination and thus were favourable to the production of new ideas, whereas analytical techniques were seen as those which simply laid emphasis on analysing a situation.

On this basis, some techniques could be clearly identified as creative in nature, for example brainstorming, and some techniques were clearly analytical, for example market analysis. But with many techniques such a clear distinction was not possible, as the techniques embraced both creative and analytical elements. Thus the findings of this part of the research depend on the subjective (if experienced) viewpoint of the author as to which category each of the techniques primarily belongs. In order that the reader may judge for himself the validity of the author's assessment, a list of the techniques and their classification as either primarily creative or primarily analytical in nature is included in Appendix 1.

However, having stated this limitation on validity, it can be said that there was a bias towards the value of creative techniques as compared with the analytical. These techniques generated over a two-year time period an average of 7.8 products per technique as compared with 6.3 products for the analytical. Also, they were marginally better rated by the companies responding than the analytical techniques.

In practice, however, the analytical techniques as a group were used by a higher proportion of companies than were the creative. One can only assume that this is because the analytical type of technique is generally both easier to understand and operate than a technique which is creative in nature.

The findings did indicate that there were at least two creative techniques and two analytical techniques which deserved to be used by a higher proportion of companies that those currently using them. These were:

Creative   — Marketing think tank
            — Consumer depth interviews
Analytical — Segmentation analysis
            — Gap analysis

CONCLUSION

It is difficult to generalize when comparing the findings of the four research studies. The studies vary in scope and content. In addition, two cover only grocery products, one covers all consumer products and one is concerned with both consumer and industrial products. Moreover, the terms used to identify a source or a technique vary between the studies. However, some sources and techniques in various forms are common to at least three of the four studies, for example market study, competition, R and D, and overseas. Others are common to two of the four studies. On this basis it is possible for a new products manager to examine the range of techniques and identify those which would appear to be of the most value in his particular company and market situation.

REFERENCES

1 Parnes S J, 'Effects of extended effort in creative problem solving', *Journal of Educational Psychology*, Vol 52, 1961.
2 Bouchard T J, 'A comparison of two brainstorming procedures', *Journal of Applied Psychology*, Vol 56, 1972.
3 Greenhalgh C, 'Generating new product ideas', *Admap*, Sept, Oct, Nov 1971.
4 Mandry G D, *New Product Development in the UK Grocery Trade*, Research Paper No 2, Retail Outlets Research Unit, Manchester Business School, 1973.
5 Randall G, *Managing New Products*, British Institute of Management, 1980.
6 Sowrey J T, *Idea Generation: The Sourcing of Ideas for New Products in Consumer Markets*, Doctoral thesis, University of Strathclyde, 1984.

Chapter 8 Conclusions

A few companies are good at new product development but I believe that 90 per cent of companies are quite dreadful at it.[1]

INTRODUCTION

One of the main conclusions of the study undertaken by Parker (1980)[2] for the British Institute of Management was that while most companies agree that new products sustain growth, few companies seriously encourage innovation.

ORGANIZATIONAL FACTORS

To bring about a more positive approach it appears to be necessary, as outlined in Chapter 3, to establish a suitable organizational structure to handle development. Such a structure is important for two reasons.

In the first place, it is almost inevitable in a company that the short-term needs of the day-to-day business will dominate the available time and resources. A conscious effort has to be made to look after the future, as no one will undertake this responsibility unless it is specifically allocated to them. Thus it is essential to designate a certain body of people to be responsible for innovation in relation to future needs. The support and involvement of top management with this body of people will further emphasize the importance of looking to the future. If top management is committed to development then everyone else in the company will be committed.

Second, the correct organizational framework can provide an environment where the personality traits of a creative person can best be accommodated, as development activities appear to benefit from a high level of creative thinking. Towards this end, the structure itself can foster creativity through the establishment of informal working relationships under a high quality leader who encourages face-to-face participation in discussion and decision making.

THE IMPORTANCE OF PLANNING

To give impetus to the work of this development organization it is necessary to establish a firm development policy. Again, such a requirement is important for two reasons.

First, the policy will provide direction in terms of a long-term strategy on where the company is going, for it should embrace overall objectives, growth goals and the way to growth. Resulting from this will be the identification of criteria to guide the search for and the evaluation of markets and product ideas compatible with the company's resources.

In the second place, a firm development policy will encourage creative thinking. The market and environmental data and consumer research on which such a policy is based will provide the basic knowledge that the creative mind requires to work on, in the process of searching for and building new combinations.

THE FRAMEWORK FOR THE SEARCH PROCESS

In order to generate ideas, the creative search should be organized and not left to chance. As discussed in Chapter 7, there is evidence that a large number of ideas appear to be necessary if a company is to succeed in launching new products. Moreover, the effectiveness of subsequent stages in the development process is entirely dependent on the idea generation stage.

The Booz, Allen and Hamilton study[3] indicated that the efficiency of companies with regard to product development varied between zero and 84 per cent. With efficiency defined as the percentage of development expenses devoted to successful rather than to unsuccessful products, then on average 70 per cent of the expenses of the companies in that study were wasted, as they were spent on unsuccessful products. To avoid this waste it is necessary to focus heavy attention on the idea generation stage, so that enough quality ideas will pass through the subsequent stages.

The approach towards instituting an idea generation system should be methodical. The objective should be the establishment of an organized network that operates on a continuous basis which embraces a central collection point and organized collection procedures. Method so applied is not a guarantee of success as there is no substitute for creative ideas, but method can organize and encourage creative thinking.

Emphasis within the network should be on quantity, that is to produce as many ideas as possible – good, bad and indifferent. It has been argued[4] that the problem is not to obtain ideas but obtain 'good' ideas, that is ideas that meet the company's objectives and have the market potential to be successful new products. This may be true, but with the right quantity and suitable procedures the right quality will emerge. The danger is that if only a small number of ideas are produced then decisions might be made, under real-life pressures, to progress low quality ideas. Such decisions would probably never be made if more suitable ideas were available.

To produce ideas in quantity it is advisable to utilize a wide range of techniques. These should seek ideas from both inside and outside the company, as both sources can be productive of ideas. In the specific environment of a company, some of the techniques will be more effective than others and it is difficult to forecast in advance which in particular will produce the best results. It was suggested in Chapter 7 that a company which uses a considerable number of techniques is more likely to develop successful new products than one which does not. As a result, it is perhaps better to start by using as many techniques as possible and then drop the ones which in practice appear to be unproductive.

In relation to the type of techniques used, as discussed in Chapter 7, there is reason to believe that some companies still fail to recognize the creative nature of the development process, relying primarily on a research-based analysis of existing product and market situations to obtain ideas. As a result techniques which are creativity-based are neglected, although ideas for successful products are perhaps a little more likely to arise from this type of technique. A sequential approach using analytical techniques may be valid but it tends to ignore the value of a creative input to idea generation. It is a question of balance and perhaps too many companies over the last decade have been either suspicious of 'irrational creativity' or alternatively, over-influenced by the quantitative approach to management. As a result they have gone a little too far in their adoption of a 'scientific' approach.

THE CONTINGENCY APPROACH

New product development, like any other activity, depends on doing the right thing if it is to be successful, but there is no magic formula. The 'classic' formula or six-stage programme for development as a whole was discussed in Chapter 5. In addition, it has been suggested in this chapter that a formula or common set of principles exists specifically in relation to idea generation. To summarize, this formula recognizes that:

1. The adoption of a suitable organizational structure and planning procedures can lead to more effective idea generation.
2. The process of generation should not be left to chance but method applied and a system organized on a continuous basis with a central collection point and collection procedures.
3. Within the system the aim should be to produce ideas in quantity on the basis that the right quality will emerge.

4. To this end the system should embrace a wide range of techniques, seeking ideas from both inside and outside the company.
5. Emphasis should be laid on creativity-oriented techniques as well as those that are analytical in character.

However, the complexity of the business environment and the variety of companies that compete in this environment ensure that this formula cannot be followed slavishly. Common principles concerning idea generation can be identified, just as basic principles in relation to the development process as a whole have been established. But a company that wishes to be successful should adopt the contingency approach, whereby it follows the common set of principles but adapts these to its own circumstances.

Over the years, management theory has taken divergent paths. The traditional and classical approach has been supplanted, or perhaps supplemented would be more appropriate, by the behaviourist, the systems and the quantitative approaches. Singly, none of these theories can be applied to every organization and to every management problem. As a result, contingency theory has emerged as an approach that can be used to draw the disparate elements together, for this approach recognizes the complexities involved in managing modern organizations that are affected by major contingencies. These contingencies embrace both external and internal constraints and influences, and include the character and diversity of environments in which the company operates, its scale of operations, plant technologies, resources and the type of people it employs. Thus, basic to contingency theory is the recognition that there is no single design that is best for all situations and that it is necessary to match classical, behavioural, systems and quantitative approaches with appropriate situational factors.

The first step in the application of contingency theory is a situational analysis. This requires a description of the organization and the environment and from this the establishment of critical variables. As applied to new products, this analysis should already take place in the planning stage as an integral part of the development process. The determination of company strengths and weaknesses and the evaluation of markets, as discussed in Chapter 4, leads to the identification of critical variables in terms of the organization and the environment and allows a company to establish a firm policy for that development.

Thus, the same factors that are examined with the purpose of establishing development objectives can have wider significance as a situational review of the organization and it environment prior to the application of contingency theory. Seen in this wider context, the review can lead not only to clear growth goals and the way to growth, but also to the appropriate organizational structure, the identification of the development stages critical to the company's operation and in many cases to the techniques most appropriate for the generation of new product concepts.

For example, a large, highly formalized company might find it necessary to create a department separate from its existing business to handle development, in order to allow for more flexible responses to be made to changes in the environment. To take this further, Child (1977)[5] illustrates how a very large organization entering a dynamic environmental field may find a need to create a separate, small subsidiary operation to deal with the new area, that is to create venture management units. A small firm, however, with loose, informal, organic arrangements and with limited resources may be satisfied that its existing structure is well able to cope with the extra demands involved with innovative strategies. Similarly, a company dominant in a stable market also may find that development is best handled within its existing structure. In general, it would appear that the bigger and more formalized the organization and the more dynamic and competitive the environment, the more it appears to be a necessity to create a structure to handle development which is separate from the existing business.

As further illustration, there may be a need for a company to adopt a very formalized approach to development if it is entering a highly competitive market. In this formalized approach, every stage in the development process is conducted thoroughly and meticulously in order that any possible risk may be minimized. On the other hand, as outlined by Sowrey (1977),[6] a company with strong pressures emanating either from within the organization or from the environment, or both, that result in constraints in relation to time may find it necessary to adopt a more flexible approach and omit certain stages in order to progress, accepting as a result its own apparently 'imperfect marketing'.

With regard to idea generation, a large company with adequate manpower resources may be able to establish a very comprehensive system which seeks ideas from many sources. At the other extreme, for a small company with limited manpower it may be advisable, at least initially, to concentrate on those techniques which have proved to be of value to other companies, as reviewed in Chapter 7. This would need to be a conscious policy, for it appears from the fourth study in Chapter 7 that the techniques which are most used in practice are not necessarily those which have proved to be of the most value. As suggested earlier, for the majority of companies it would probably be advisable to utilize as many techniques as possible and at a later stage drop the ones which have proved to be the least fruitful.

CONCLUSION

In adopting the contingency approach to development, it is essential that a company recognizes that a common set of principles exists in relation to idea generation and the development process as a whole. Then, following a situational analysis, it will be in the position to adapt these principles to its own operation. As a result, it may be necessary to accept some compromise with regard to the theoretical ideal, in terms of organizational structure and development activities. This may mean the acceptance of a degree of theoretical imperfection in its approach and an acceptance of a larger degree of risk. In addition, it also requires an awareness that the organization and its environment change over time and that, as a result, there is a need periodically to review the company's development policies in relation to the contingency approach, and further adapt where necessary. But by recognizing that the basic principles are the starting point for the application of contingency theory, a company is adopting a positive attitude to development. The danger is that there may be a failure to recognize the common set of principles, with the result that the company deviates from these principles out of ignorance rather than from design. Such an unplanned approach can only lead to an ineffective development policy.

The need to recognize that a common set of principles exist applies in particular to idea generation. It applies to this stage simply because so little has been written on the subject that the basic principles have not clearly emerged. Baty[7] stated in 1963 that, 'few useful principles have been advanced to show companies how best to use their resources to generate a flow of new ideas'. In the mid-1980s the situation appears to be still the same. 'Other stages of new product development have been refined into almost routine-like necessity but both practitioners and academics continue to struggle with different methods for idea generation.'[8] Therefore it is to this end that this book has been written and it is hoped that the conclusions arrived at in this chapter can serve as a common set of principles for the idea generation stage. Now, more than ever, it is essential that companies should, 'search for new product ideas . . . without this vital entrepreneurial outlook few firms can expect to prosper in the knife edge competition of modern markets'.[9]

REFERENCES

1 Krausher P M, Paper presented to an Advertising Association Conference, reported in *Marketing Week*, 3 November 1981.
2 Parker R C, *Guidelines for Product Innovation*, British Institute of Management, 1980.
3 Booz, Allen and Hamilton Inc, *The Management of New Products*, 1966.
4 Pollitt S, 'A practical approach to new products and new concepts', *Admap*, March 1970.

5 Child J, 'Organisational design and performance – contingency theory and beyond', *Organisation and Administrative Studies*, August 1977.
6 Sowrey J T, 'The theory of imperfect marketing', *The Quarterly Review of Marketing*, Summer 1977.
7 Baty G B, 'Generating a flow of new product ideas', *Machine Design*, July 1963.
8 Fornell C and Menko R D, 'Problem analysis: a consumer based methodology for the discovery of new product ideas', *European Journal of Marketing*, Vol 15, No 5, 1981.
9 Chisnall P M, 'Marketing research techniques for generating new consumer products', *Supplement to the Market Research Society Newsletter*, No 168, March 1980.

Chapter 9 Development in Action

INTRODUCTION

There is no doubt that the inclusion of case studies improves any book concerned with marketing theory, as it enables the reader to see how companies have applied the theory in real-life situations. The need for case illustration is especially relevant when considering new product development policies, as concentrated external and internal pressures on a company can result in a situation where the gap between theory and practice is probably wider than in any other aspect of marketing. In this particular book, case studies also help to illustrate the contingency approach outlined in the previous chapter, and the need to follow a common set of principles but adapt them to the peculiar circumstances of the company and its market.

But obtaining case material in the development area is difficult. Indeed, in examining any book devoted entirely to case studies one is fortunate to find even a single case that illustrates an aspect of new product development.

The reason for this is the negative attitude most companies adopt with regard to divulging information on their development activities. This is perfectly understandable; an aura of secrecy surrounds these activities for fear that competitors may learn something of value. In addition, company managers might be inhibited in providing information for fear that the portrayal of that information could reflect unfavourably on the reputation of their company. As a result, the need to preserve anonymity is paramount when attempting to gather case material on development activities.

In this chapter three case studies are presented. One concerns a company that adopted a marketing-oriented approach to its development activities, another a company that was trying to do so, but unsuccessfully, and another a company that was trying to do so and succeeded. Whatever the extent of marketing orientation depicted there is something to be learnt from each case, for with new product development it is extremely hard not to make a mistake of one kind or another. The difference between success and failure depends on the gravity of the mistake and the number of mistakes that are made.

For the reasons stated above, anonymity is preserved in two of these case studies and the companies concerned, although household names, are simply referred to as company A and company B. The author was personally involved in the launch described in the third case study and the company has previously given permission for the material to be published in an article.[1] The case described in this chapter is based on that article.

COMPANY A: A NEW BISCUIT PRODUCT

The market

The biscuit market is certainly no stranger to new product launches and not long ago company A introduced a new biscuit into a specific segment of that market. The total market is a large one and at the time of the launch it was approximately £500 million at retail selling prices, totally supplied by UK manufacturers and highly competitive, with six major manufacturers and a number of smaller companies. Two of these manufacturers accounted for over 60 per cent of sales between them. Although stable in total, the market had considerable fluctuations relating to particular segments. Company A launched its product into an expanding market segment dominated by the brand leader. In order to preserve the anonymity of company A, the segment will be referred to in this case study as the 'fruit' biscuit market segment.

The company

Like all the major biscuit manufacturers company A sold a wide range of food products, but biscuits were very important to overall profitability. Its plant was highly automated because of the need to keep product costs as low as possible in this very competitive market, and the company possessed a high level of knowledge and skills among managers in all the main departmental areas. The level of marketing expertise in particular was sophisticated, as indeed it would have to be to compete in one of the largest grocery food markets.

Organization

The whole of the development team, both marketing and R and D, reported to the marketing director who was a member of the board. In the new products manager, reporting direct to the marketing director, the company had a member of the marketing staff working full time on new products, with line extensions to existing products being the responsibility of the brand groups. The R and D sections based at the factories were responsible to the R and D manager at head office who in turn, for new products, was responsible to the marketing director.

This form of organization was established because the board of directors felt that there was a need to pay greater attention to development. The organizational structure previously in existence, whereby development was handled by the existing products brand groups, had been perceived as too unwieldy. Indeed, as discussed in Chapter 3, this is a normal form of progression as development activities increase. Thus, the board of directors had taken action when it was necessary and development had the board's full and committed support. But there was a qualification, in that hitherto the board had been concerned totally with establishing a good profit record from the existing product range and their conversion to the need to invest in development had come late.

There was no doubt that the production director was a firm supporter of development, which is often not the case with production personnel, but the situation was not always harmonious between marketing and production, as negative attitudes sometimes arose from the latter in an attempt to prevent disruption to existing planned production schedules. However, the production director did support new products and could get things done and the marketing staff very much appreciated his support.

Planning

A few years before the launch, the company had formally put on to paper for the first time a corporate plan covering a five-year time period and this was updated annually. The plan was primarily compiled by members of the board, although they in turn were provided with specific input from the staff in their own departments.

This plan followed the 'classic' format, in that in addition to sales, expenditure and profit forecasts it embraced a statement of corporate objectives and strategy. In addition, development objectives were included with sales and profit targets which could be stated in general terms or related to a specific product if the development of that product had progressed to the final stages. The development objectives and sales and profit targets for new products originated with the new products manager. As a result of the completion of the necessary basic groundwork to arrive at these objectives, a sense of direction compatible with the company's resources was given to the development policy. In this particular case, that direction pointed simply towards the establishment, at minimum capital investment cost, of a new brand on a profitable basis that would enhance the company's position in the total biscuit market.

A programme

A 'classic' approach was also adopted in relation to the development of new products, which again indicated the level of marketing orientation of the company. Screening and financial evaluation of ideas, concept and product tests were all part of a formalized programme. Area test markets were not carried out, but for valid reasons, the problem of getting some of the national accounts in the grocery trade to co-operate (eg Sainsbury) could make an area test impractical. Instead of an area test market, some form of mini test was used, usually selling the product nationally through a selected customer group.

The search process

One vital stage, however, was omitted in this formalized programme, that of idea generation. The search for new ideas, to quote a member of the development team, 'took place informally'. In his eyes, the company adopted the 'easy approach of immediate opportunities' that arrive informally and no one within the company had ever pressed for an organized idea generation system, simply because a lack of manpower acted as a major constraint. As a result, most of the development team were not satisfied with the quantity and quality of ideas that arose in the company.

Where, then, did the ideas come from? As indicated above, they arose in an *ad hoc* manner rather than from an organized search. As a result, they were primarily for 'me too' products and were unlikely to result in anything truly innovative. The main sources were in-house – from personnel in marketing, R and D and production. Also, a few ideas had come in the past from sister companies abroad, overseas travel, outside consultants, market analysis, competition and trade magazines.

The new biscuit: idea generation

The development and launch of the new biscuit had the full and complete commitment of the company and as a project was handled with a sophisticated, marketing-oriented approach. Where the idea for the product actually came from was not absolutely clear, but the new product that finally emerged in the market place appeared to have been shaped by preconceived ideas, regardless of what transpired from any idea-generating techniques or consumer research.

The new biscuit: a programme

The first stage in developing a viable new product was a concept test in which several biscuit concepts (including a 'fruit' biscuit) devised by marketing and R and D were tested among office staff in the company. The concepts were represented by prototype biscuit products because it was felt that no concept could be adequately represented for a biscuit unless it was actually tasted. In fact, all the biscuits failed.

Then several months later, in conjunction with a research company specializing in synectics, a two-day synectics problem workshop was held. The objective of the workshop, based on the brief given by the company, was to devise at least six new biscuit product concepts. The group consisted of five of the company managers involved in development (from marketing, R and D, production and engineering), two housewives and two members of the research company. The latter two conducted the workshop using the synectics problem-solving skills and procedures. As a result, 10 separate concepts arose and, as dictated by the brief, all were broadly similar to a 'fruit' type of biscuit although they did not specifically include a 'fruit' biscuit.

From these 10 concepts it proved possible to develop five biscuit products within R and D. These were tested in four group discussions among housewives, two groups being in London and two in the Midlands. Although the five concepts in general were found to be acceptable by the groups, the biscuits themselves were again rejected because of a lack of taste and flavour.

Further R and D work then concentrated on the one most favoured concept and while this development work was taking place, four group discussions were held among suburban housewives in London to identify the most acceptable shape for the new product and to help establish the biscuit's positioning in the market.

However, it appears that the product that finally emerged from R and D development was specifically a 'fruit' biscuit. This was tested in-hall among a sample of 450 housewives in London and Manchester. The test was based on monadic and paired comparison tests against the brand leader in the 'fruit' biscuit market segment and it was very well accepted, with good scores achieved against the brand leader.

It had taken two years of development from the concept test to reach this point. By this stage there was no doubt that the new product was seen within the company as a 'fruit' biscuit. It is possible that the type of biscuit developed by R and D determined future events, as it was so obviously a 'fruit' biscuit in character. But so far as actual product development is concerned it is more likely that they were working to a firm brief and that the marketing team had already made up its mind, if only informally, as to the type of biscuit required.

A justification for entering the 'fruit' biscuit market appeared in the marketing launch plan, written some six months later. This justification was perfectly logical and valid and not simply a rationalization to justify action already taken. But the importance of the 'fruit' biscuit segment of the market appears to have exerted involuntary but compulsive pressures on individuals that dictated from the earliest development stages, without any formal decision ever having been made, the character and positioning of the new biscuit. This happened over a two-year period of time, regardless of any other factors, in particular the results of consumer research.

The hall test of the new biscuit was followed by an in-home placement test among a sample of 400 housewives in London and Manchester. The objective was to assess the total product offering, that is the packaged product with brand name, at a given price and weight. Monadic and paired comparison tests were used on three calls at the home. At the first two calls two packets were placed (the new product and the brand leader) and at the third call just one packet (a free offer of either the new product or the brand leader). The results were judged to be favourable and a 'go' decision made to launch in the following April or May.

The new biscuit: the launch

To guide the final stages of the development process, that is the preparation for launch, it was decided to set up a project group consisting of seven key people who would be involved in the launch of the product. These seven people represented marketing, R and D, production, quality control, production engineering, work study and sales. Project groups had been used by the company before, but on a far more limited scale.

The work of the project group was based around network planning to cover a period of seven months up to launch. The critical path led to production commencing in February for a launch date in April or May. However, production was delayed for a month because of shelf life problems that arose. This necessitated further development work followed by consumer tests in-hall. But with trade receptions in March, followed by a sales conference to allow pre-selling to the trade, the official launch did occur in April. This launch was fully national. No test market was held; this was a risk and contingency plans were drawn up to minimize that risk should the product not fulfil expectations.

The programme of R and D work and consumer testing had taken three years to complete from the concept test to the final launch. Now was felt to be the right time for launch, as the consumer research results were good and it was believed that the product would be acceptable to the trade. But above all, it was felt that a test market would have warned competition and brought a strong reaction in the market place which would have endangered the possibility of achieving a successful national extension.

The marketing objective for the first year of launch was to achieve a specific brand share for the product. The strategy to achieve this objective laid emphasis on a product which was equal to competition on key product dimensions but with a strong image differentiation. Heavy television advertising was used as the prime means of gaining trade distribution and in-home penetration, with secondary support from trade incentives, in-store demonstrations and point of sale material. The television advertising which commenced in August, that is four months after the launch date to enable distribution to be gained, was strongly theme based and 60 per cent of total expenditure went on this medium in order to achieve 600 television rating points (TVRs) in a four-week burst in August/September, which was followed by a four-week burst in the spring. Sterling distribution targets were 60 to 65 per cent nationally after four months and an in-home penetration was aimed at 5 per cent monthly after the initial advertising burst.

This launch was a success, but in the eyes of company managers the success was qualified in that the marketing objective had not quite been met. One year after launch, the brand share achieved was 3 per cent below target and this was obtained from a low level of sterling distribution after four months and a low level of in-home penetration. However, after 16 months, in spite of a heavy counter-attack from competition the brand share was only 1 per cent beneath target, although still from a low level of distribution and in-home penetration.

Summary

Company A possessed a high level of marketing expertise, recognizing and being familiar with the framework and principles relating to new product development. As a large company with a multiple range of branded consumer goods, competing in highly competitive grocery markets, it adopted the product management system to organize its marketing activities. But to avoid the danger of new products being neglected it had separated development from existing products under a new products manager, although line extensions remained the responsibility of the product managers. The danger of neglect had been found to be a problem at a time when new products had been the responsibility of product managers.

R and D was responsible to marketing and not – as is often the case – to production, thus further minimizing the danger of a neglect of development work. As in many companies, the 'classic confrontation' between marketing and production was in evidence but this was mitigated by the fact that the production director, by reason of his background experience, was a supporter of development. This support was encouraged by marketing through the mechanism of project groups, and the group formed for the launch of the new 'fruit' biscuit played an important part, with the help of network planning, in bringing about a successful launch.

New products also had the committed support of the board of directors and corporate planning was carried out with managers beneath board level being involved, as well as the directors. Development objectives were part of this plan, giving a direction to activities. The company participated in highly competitive, sophisticated markets and as mistakes could be costly, a formalized programme was adopted for the development of new products, including the new 'fruit' biscuit. But the company neglected one stage in its development programme, that of idea generation. No organized search system was in existence. This was attributable to the lack of attention paid to new products by top management in the past, resulting in a lack of investment in manpower in this area.

As a result, the company had few good ideas that could be progressed through the development process. At this point in time there was only one and if that failed at some stage in development, then there were no other good ideas to progress. This insecurity appeared to give rise to a degree of procrastination among managers and it could be argued that if a clear initial decision had been made to develop a new 'fruit' biscuit for this expanding market segment, then the long gestation period involving repeated product reformulations and consumer research tests might have been considerably shortened.

COMPANY B: A NEW TOY

The market

New products are the lifeblood of the market for toys and a high proportion are bought by the consumer in the ten weeks prior to Christmas. It is this brief period of time that accounts for over 50 per cent of volume sales. The product introduced by company B was aimed at this pre-Christmas period when peak consumer purchases occur.

At the time of the launch, the market was worth around £650 million at retail selling prices. It was then, and still is, a very fragmented industry, with severe competition embracing over 700 manufacturers in the UK as well as imported products. At the time 11 companies dominated, with a share of over 70 per cent. Then, as now, the market had the characteristics of a fashion industry and was highly volatile in nature. Although new products are important in any market, they are of paramount importance in so capricious a market as that of toys.

The company

The company is a subsidiary of a major group operating internationally. There was only one production unit within the company and this was very simply based on the processing of paper. Components made of other materials, such as plastic or electronic units, had to be bought in and where necessary assembled with the components derived from paper.

Overall, there were considerable variations among managers in the level of knowledge and skills in the main departmental areas. This was not a variation between one department and another but between individuals within a department. This was partly attributable to the fact that the company had brought in a number of able people from outside, which resulted in a mixture of old and new personnel within any one department.

Organization

Because of the very nature of the development process in company B there was no separate R and D unit. Product prototypes were easily assembled, as they consisted of paper, board, plastic and metal components and microchip units and combinations thereof. Thus, the marketing department was also responsible for the production of prototypes, calling on the help of outside design studios where necessary.

Although the department was responsible for both existing and new products, the fashion nature of the industry entailed that the development of new products occupied most of their working time and, indeed, most of the marketing budget.

A new organizational structure for the department had been established for some 12 months. The structure previously in existence split responsibility for new products from existing products, but this proved to be unworkable as personality problems had resulted in a lack of liaison between the two marketing sections. Personality problems continued to be important, but this time between marketing and other departments, and the marketing team were aware of criticisms. But with the new organizational structure, some barriers had begun to break down.

Planning

Corporate planning was undertaken to cover a three-year time period, but each director separately covered his area of responsibility and as a result the plan lacked unity. In addition, few, if any, managers below director level were involved and thus the plan also lacked depth.

A business plan covering one year was also produced. Here, the planning process did involve managers beneath board level. The marketing section of the plan gave an indication of marketing strategy in addition to sales objectives. From this stemmed the separate plans for the operating areas. The marketing strategy was simply 'to find a niche in the market' through the development of new products.

A programme

The fashion nature of the industry, with the constant need for new products to be available to show the trade at the turn of each year, does inhibit to some extent the adoption of a systematic development programme. But the programme within company B was conducted on a very informal basis. The screening of ideas took place at the monthly marketing meetings, but in a subjective manner rather than against an objective checklist. Financial evaluation took place at the prototype stage, on the basis of sales and profit forecasts for one year only. The use of concept and product tests was very limited. When such a test did take place it usually took the form of a concept test, using a product prototype among groups of children (and their parents) from local schools. This would be arranged by the advertising agency or a design consultant and not by a specialist market research company. The nature of the business restricted the use of test marketing, although occasionally a mini-test through selected outlets might be arranged.

The search process

A development programme of this type has no room for an organized search process and all ideas came informally and not from a search. A few outside sources were used – unsolicited ideas from the general public and from professional and semi-professional inventors and products under licence from companies outside the UK – but most of the good ideas were in-house, in that they came personally from the marketing director. Thus, there was too great a reliance on just one individual and the rest of the marketing team assumed the role of implementers without being heavily involved in trying to source ideas themselves.

In this particular industry, more than most, there is a critical need for ideas because toys have a short product life cycle which is on average three years. But every manufacturer would like to develop a toy to bridge the generation gap, in that the appeal of the product would be strong enough for parents who had enjoyed it as children then to buy it for their children, who in turn would buy it eventually for their own children.

Success for a product could be judged from two standpoints. A product could be a success at a fairly low sales level if its life was above average, in that it was on the market from four to 10 years. On the other hand, a product with a short life of one to four years had to achieve a much higher sales volume. To achieve both a long life cycle and a high sales volume, a product should follow a fashion trend in the market and in addition have a high degree of 'play value' which would carry it beyond the fashion. One essential element for success also was that the product must be advertised. This was not only for the purpose of stimulating consumer sales, but to obtain trade acceptance.

In the toy industry the trade have a tremendous influence, as they expect new toys from manufacturers every year. If you cannot get their support, a product is just not viable. Moreover, at the sell-in to the trade, one year before the consumer sales peak at Christmas, they have a tremendous choice. Thus, it is essential to have a variety of new products to offer the trade.

The new toy: idea generation

The idea for the new toy launched by company B arose internally. The company had established a working relationship with a supplier of microchips in the Far East, as a result of using chip technology in an earlier product. They were approached by the supplier with a new facility based on microchip technology. Nothing was done with this new facility at this stage. Then four months later, after a decision had been made to enter the pre-school segment of the market (children three to five years) the new microchip facility was examined again. The company did not have a product in this market segment and with rising birth trends this was now a growth area. In order to create a toy with play value it was decided to add cardboard and plastic pieces, and a design consultancy was commissioned to supply the ideas and designs for the form which these should take.

The new toy: a programme

The design consultancy set up a concept test to obtain an indication of the acceptability of the new toy that had been created around the chip facility and the cardboard and plastic additions. Group discussions involving children and their parents took place, using a prototype product. It was felt that the test showed that the concept was acceptable, particularly as parents liked the toy as they looked on it as semi-constructional. But the product did not appear to be in quite the right format, as it had not enough play value for the children. New cardboard designs were required in order to achieve this. The new cardboard additions were devised internally by the marketing department. However, these could not be tested in a product test as time was too short if the product was to be available, as planned, for a preview to the trade in November and the sales conference in December. The annual catalogue had to be ready for printing by October if it was to be available for the conference.

The advertising agents were asked to supply names that could be tested but, again, because of shortage of time the testing did not take place. In fact, it was decided that the internal code name that had been used to identify the product would be used as the brand name. A guide to pricing had been incorporated into the concept test as a price band and it was decided to price the product at the top of this band. The time factor also did not permit any form of market test.

The new toy: the launch

The product was presented at the trade preview held by the company in November. This took the form of an invited audience of major buyers, who were shown the company's range of new products for sale to the consumer prior to Christmas in the following year. Two centres were used for the trade preview, one in London and one in the north of England. The former was primarily for the retail buyers, such as Boots, W H Smith and Woolworths, and the latter primarily for mail order houses. Trade reaction was favourable and the product was launched officially at the sales conference in December. This was followed by exhibition at the toy fair in Harrogate and Earls Court early in the new year.

Sales to the trade on a period-by-period analysis from the new year onwards were judged to be good, as were the findings of the distribution checks that a research company was commissioned to carry out. Television advertising was to commence prior to Christmas with a budget to achieve 100 child TVRs and 60 adult TVRs. Thus, it was confidently expected that the product would be a major success.

But consumer sales immediately prior to Christmas were disappointing. Indeed, so much so that the product was regarded as a failure. In the early stages of development there had been some reservations expressed by sales management concerning the price of the product. It was felt that it might be seen as too high by consumers for what was essentially a toy made of cardboard. Now the pricing policy was seen by management as the reason for failure. However, it could appear to an outsider to the company that failure might have been avoided if the product had been adequately research tested.

Summary

Company B was relatively unsophisticated in the area of marketing when compared with many companies operating in other packaged goods markets, such as the grocery market. The products had a very strong seasonality which imposed time constraints on the annual marketing programme. This programme was oriented towards the development of new products for launch by the end of each year. As a result, most of the marketing activity was devoted to development. Accordingly, the form of organization adopted was for the marketing team to handle both development and existing products. An organization which separated the control of new products from existing products had been tried but had proved to be unworkable. As no particular technical expertise was required in product formulation this was the responsibility of the marketing team, and there was no R and D section.

Development had the full support of the board of company B. However, this commitment was comparatively recent and for many years only slight attention had been paid to the need for new products, until competitive pressures emphasized that need.

But the company was not committed to adequate corporate planning and as a result there appeared to be a lack of clear direction for the development policy. This direction appeared to be no more than to find a niche in the market, without that niche being clearly defined and with no firm policy on how to find it.

The time constraints that resulted from the nature of the market were an inhibiting influence on the adoption of a systematic development programme, but the lack of a definite corporate policy was perhaps a stronger influence preventing such an adoption. However, for whatever reason, no systematic programme was in existence. As a result there appeared to be too great a reliance on one man, the marketing director, to supply ideas for new products.

Once an idea arose and was progressed, there was usually a lack of consumer research testing. Test markets are not possible where the trade are unlikely to co-operate and where plagiarism by competitors is an ever present danger. Thus, the need for consumer research testing is very much apparent. Undoubtedly time constraints were again an inhibiting influence, but a longer product gestation period with time allowed for adequate testing would probably have been more appropriate. However, the lack of experience in handling a research programme and the inadequate criteria against which products could be measured, which resulted from the lack of a clear policy, were further constraints in this respect.

Thus it is not surprising that with the launch of the new toy the company should think that it had a winner and then find that it had not.

COURAGE BREWING LTD: COLT 45 MALT LIQUOR

The market

The beer market in Britain is one of tradition. Indeed, what appears to matter most to the man in the street is that his pint of bitter be preserved just as it is. This certainly means no metric pots and no Common Market beers brewed from the same recipe.

To introduce a new drink, and such a contradictory type of drink as Colt 45, into the huge, traditional beer market was no mean feat in 1973. The UK was then, as now, the third largest market in the world after the USA and West Germany. In size it was around £2,250 million at retail selling prices. Draught beer dominated, accounting for 69 per cent of the total, with the remainder split between bottles at 22 per cent and cans at 9 per cent. The majority of beer was drunk, of course, in the pub situation, as it is today.

Some changes in the drinking habits of the UK population had affected the nature of the market. Dark mild beers had lost popularity to bitters and lagers. Lager, in particular, had grown virtually from nothing to 18 per cent of the total market. Canned beer had also grown considerably, due to the readiness of people to take beer home to drink and, as a result, beer was stocked by grocers as well as the established off-licence trade. The consumer profile of the public house had also changed. For a long time, pubs were dominated by the middle-aged man, but younger age groups and both sexes began to be regular pub customers. Pubs adopted a more modern appearance as brewers raced to capitalize on, and indeed encourage, this trend. Discos, live entertainment, juke boxes, intimate lighting, snacks at the bar and restaurant facilities became common.

The company

Perhaps the biggest change in the market was the gradual concentration of supply into fewer hands. Once every area had its own brewer but, after a process of mergers and takeovers, the market became dominated by the big eight, of which Courage was one. These eight companies also included Bass Charrington, Whitbread, Allied, Watney, Scottish and Newcastle, Greenall Whitley and Guinness. Between them they accounted for 80 per cent of the UK trade. Guinness stood alone in that it owned no pubs but distributed its unique beer to all other brewers.

Organization

Like many other brewers at that time, the establishment of a marketing department had been of comparatively recent origin. Apart from sales personnel it embraced only five people and they were responsible for both existing and new products. Because it was small and the workload was so great it tended to operate organically, with only tenuous demarcation lines separating job responsibilities.

Planning

The Courage group of companies was a large group, embracing several companies operating in different fields. Any corporate planning that was done took place outside the scope of the brewery company marketing department. Within that department, a marketing plan was produced on an annual basis.

A programme and the search process

As a result of the heavy workload brought by existing products the approach to new product development could only be described as opportunistic.

Colt 45: idea generation

Colt 45 presented the Courage brewery marketing department with an opportunity. But what is Colt 45 malt liquor? Simply it is a beer without hops – and thus not strictly speaking a beer – that has a mild taste, a sort of gentle cross between lager, cider and wine. Colt 45 is strong, with an original gravity higher than the average pint of bitter. It can be summed up in a phrase full of contradictions as a bland, alcoholic, soft drink-type beer designed to appeal specifically to younger age groups.

The product idea did not result from in-depth market studies or from creative analytical techniques. Courage were simply approached by the National Brewing Corporation of Baltimore, USA, the brewers and owners of the trademark of Colt 45. National had developed the product and claimed that its success was such in the USA that sales had averaged a 21 per cent increase annually over the five preceding years. However, the various brewers they approached in Britain, offering the UK rights on the product, showed little interest. On the face of it, it did not seem a likely proposition. To begin with it was in a can, and canned beers were only drunk at home and this market, although small, was already intensely price competitive. Second, it was American, in fact and in image, and the time when American habits and fashions dominated the UK was long gone. Indeed, the trends from abroad in beer, as with other things, were then continental. Contintental lager was certainly the biggest growth sector of the UK beer market.

Colt 45: a programme

This view of Colt 45 was confirmed by qualitative group discussions held by Courage. The product was acceptable as a drink and seen as different from other drinks, but the can design and the name were old-fashioned in image and it appeared that there was a suspicion that an American beer might be of poor quality.

One answer would have been to take this acceptable drink and simply rename it and redesign the can. But Courage believed that the beer would stand or fall in the UK by its concept, of which the name and can design were an integral part, rather than by product acceptability alone. For it was a concept different from any other drink in the UK and had the advantage also of being youth-oriented in a traditional market lacking in products for the young. If one accepted this viewpoint, then it naturally followed that such a concept could not be adequately tested by research but must be tested against the background of persuasive advertising backing.

Although this viewpoint would appear as heresy to the writer of a marketing textbook, the next proposal appeared heresy to the traditional . brewer. For Courage management proposed to sell this canned beer in pubs. Traditionally, draught beer was drunk in pubs and canned beer was drunk at home. The very existence of canned beer had always appeared a little foolish to the brewer and it seemed madness to expect a canned beer to be drunk in the draught beer situation of a pub. However, Courage saw that there was little point in establishing Colt in so small a market as the take-home trade. Moreover, with pub sales they gained a guaranteed distribution in all Courage houses, a vital factor for any new product. Colt 45 could also attract a young drinking public into Courage pubs and against the national average of 18 per cent of pub customers in the younger age groups, the Courage pub profile had only 9 per cent.

Colt 45: the launch

Thus plans were drawn up for a test market. The product had the formidable task of having to create a new usage situation, ie canned beer drunk in public houses. This was quite a task when the product's acceptability had been indicated only by very small-scale qualitative research and when the name and can design had been seen as unacceptable.

To say the least, the test area was small by test market standards, as it encompassed only the city of Brighton. Whatever the results, they could hardly be said to be indicative of the national situation. But the test area had to be small as Courage, not wanting to finance their own plant for an unknown product, had to rely on imported stock from the National Brewing Corporation. Neither could it be said that Brighton was representative of the UK population, particularly as the test was to take place over the summer months, for the city's population would be swollen with holidaymakers and day-trippers. The visitors to Brighton, however, would be biased towards Colt's target market – ie the young – and Courage believed that with such a small-scale test they had to obtain results of sufficient volume to be analysed, thus it was felt necessary to bias the test towards the success of the product. The fact that Brighton was also strong in Courage pubs was a further bias towards success.

The test took place over the summer, with Colt being available in Courage pubs in Brighton and a number of off-licences, grocery stores and private clubs. The cinema was used for advertising because of the high proportion of young people forming the cinema audience. A hard-hitting film was used, based on the 'Godfather' theme which was then still current in popular imagination.

The whole test was a riproaring success. How much of this was due to the acceptability of the Colt 45 concept and how much to the hot summer of July and August 1973 is difficult to determine. But sales ran away with themselves and exceeded all expectations. Indeed, it had been intended originally to test in two towns, Reading as well as Brighton, but so exceptional was the demand that it was thought advisable to close the operation in Reading to avoid any possible danger of exhausting the imported stock of Colt.

In spite of the limitations of the mini-test in enabling forecasts to be made of the product's full potential, the demand for Colt was such that Courage felt they could now proceed to launch the product into London and the south-east in the summer of 1974, as the first part of a two-stage national extension. This was a key area for Courage, and indeed for the beer market as a whole. Although distributing their beers nationally, Courage had originated as a London brewer and almost 45 per cent of their public houses were situated in the proposed extension area. Thus, the extension was a substantial rolling launch rather than an extended test and required the company to invest in brewing their own Colt 45 product. Yet the general economic situation in the UK did not exactly favour investment. The planning for the extension took place during the three-day week in the winter of early 1974 and there was uncertainty about future supplies of tinplate for the cans, not only for Colt 45 but for all canned beers.

However, the pressures of reality were on Courage. The National Brewing Corporation were pressing the company to exercise their option on the sole UK rights and Bass Charrington had developed their own malt liquor called 'Breaker' which was on test in Scotland. Moreover, it was realized by the Courage marketing department that the success of the town test had lit a torch of enthusiasm for Colt among the brewery salesforce, of which it was advisable to take advantage immediately.

The product was extended into London and the south-east in the summer of 1974. Qualitative tests had been held to ensure that the Courage brew was as acceptable as the National product. But so far no full-scale tests had been held to see if the product itself was acceptable. The company simply had not had time.

The cinema, with its young audience, had been used in Brighton but cost ruled this out for the larger area and television was chosen. Unfortunately Courage were soon deprived of their Godfather film in a manner which was pure farce. Although this amusing film had proved in video tests to have a strong appeal to the public generally and although it had captured the imagination of the Courage salesforce, it had unfortunately offended a handful of people somewhere, whose letters reached the Independent Television Companies Association. One wonders how many of the writers were publicans who were unduly sensitive to the 'menacing' attitude of the mafia Godfather in making an offer of Colt 45 that could not be refused by the publican portrayed in the film. As a result, Courage thought it advisable to withdraw the film and a new commercial had to be shot.

The extension was evaluated after nine months and once again the product had been extremely successful. Sales exceeded budget and compared favourably with Courage Light Ale which had long been an established brand.

Then, in April 1975, Courage extended distribution nationally covering the west and the north of England. The product soon achieved a level of sale in the west equivalent to that achieved in London and the south, and in the north results were even more spectacular. Courage had expressed doubts about the northern market. Here bitter beer was very much an established drink among both young and old and there had been fears that Colt would not be found acceptable. But the level of sale and distribution achieved was three times that anticipated and compared most favourably with that already gained in London and the south.

Summary

Without a doubt, the launch of Colt 45 into the UK market was a success which justified the action Courage took and their belief in the product concept. Colt 45 was viewed not just as a drink but as a drink for the youth market in an established American package. It was seen by them as a product different from the range of drinks available, which in character both as a product (a mild gentle taste with body) and as a concept (an

American malt liquor) would appeal to young adults – and as events proved it did appeal to young people.

To many marketing managers the action taken by Courage may have appeared inadequate. They had gone ahead with a product whose concept has been found unacceptable, without a full-scale product test, and introduced it into an entirely new usage situation in a market steeped in tradition. On the basis of results from an unrepresentative town test with sales distorted by an exceptionally hot summer, they had extended into their major market using an advertisement and media different from that used in the test. These somewhat unusual steps were taken because of the pressures inherent in this particular situation; pressures arising from the National Brewing Corporation's desire to see quick results, from competition, and from the need at each stage of the launch to sell in during the spring or wait another year. Above all, they had pressure in the traditional brewery environment from the need to keep up momentum for the product, in case both company and trade enthusiasm should be lost. These sorts of pressure are not new – especially in a new product launch. Many companies sometimes bend the rules a little in accordance with the market situation. But the combination of pressures and the strong traditions of the beer market made the problems in the Colt launch perhaps more intense than is normal.

Thus, in following the simple theory of accepting the rules, the regrettable need to break them because of real-life pressures, the need to try and minimize the risks that followed and accepting as a result their own apparently 'imperfect' marketing, Courage successfully introduced a new type of alcoholic drink into the UK market. However, it must be admitted that good fortune was on their side. Some of the decisions that were made which were not confirmed by research turned out to be right. But they could have equally turned out to be wrong.

CONCLUSION

The three companies that have been examined varied in their levels of marketing sophistication and also in the outcome of their respective new product launches. The connection between marketing sophistication and new product success appears obvious. But it has not yet been proven by research although Project Sappho[2] and other studies have attempted to establish a link.

Because of the variations in marketing expertise, the companies naturally varied in the level of sophistication of their respective development programmes. But the three companies had one feature in common, in that none of them had established an organized search process to generate ideas for new products. As a result, all three ran into problems because the lack of ideas put pressure on the development programme for the product featured in each of the case studies.

In the end one company failed to launch a successful product, another did succeed but the result could have been quite the reverse given different circumstances, and another succeeded after wasting valuable time. But the three companies may be looked upon as the tip of an iceberg. Despite their limitations with regard to the search process each company did launch a new product on to the market. Beneath this tip there are probably many, many companies who can never be featured in a case study. They are unable to generate ideas and thus they are never in a position to launch a new product – successfully or unsuccessfully.

REFERENCES

1. Sowrey J T, 'The theory of imperfect marketing', *The Quarterly Review of Marketing*, Summer 1977.
2. Achilladelis B, Jervis P and Robertson A, *A Study of Success and Failure in Industrial Innovation*, Centre for the Study of Industrial Innovation, Sussex University, 1972.

Appendix 1 Creative and Analytical Techniques

The techniques were divided into the two groups, creative and analytical, and those which were clearly one or the other were placed in Section 1 in each group, while those which could not be so easily categorized were placed in Section 2. Because of difficulties in categorization, both an outside consultant and a supplier were omitted from consideration. (Reference: Study 4, Chapter 7.)

CREATIVE

Section 1

R and D department
Consumer group discusssions
Marketing think tank
Ideas at sales meetings
Consumer depth interviews
Brainstorming (managers)
Continuous suggestion scheme
Pseudo product test
Brainstorming (consumers)
Think tank (managers)

Section 2

Store visits
Overseas store visits
Overseas exhibitions
The advertising agency
Salesman report forms

ANALYTICAL

Section 1

Competitors' products
Market analysis
Overseas trade magazines
Trade magazines
Overseas consumer magazines
New product reports (overseas)
Past consumer research data
Overseas price lists etc
Previous ideas/projects
Gap analysis
Acquisition studies
Consumer complaints
Overseas exhibition catalogues
Product checklists
Value analysis
Trade complaints
Segmentation analysis

Section 2

Overseas sister company
Overseas manufacturers
Licensing/joint venture
Trade surveys

Appendix 2 Summary of Idea Generation Literature

BOOKS CONCERNED WITH ONE (OR A SELECTED NUMBER) OF IDEA GENERATION TECHNIQUES

Adams J L, *Conceptual Blockbusting: A Guide to Better Ideas*, Norton, 1979.
Carson J W and Rickards T, *Industrial New Product Development*, Gower 1979.
de Bono E, *The Use of Lateral Thinking*, Jonathan Cape, 1967.
de Bono E, *Lateral Thinking for Managment*, McGraw Hill, 1971.
Gordon W J J, *Synectics: the Development of Creative Capacity*, Harper and Row, 1961.
Osborn A F, *Applied Imagination*, Charles Scribners' Sons, 1957.
Parnes S J, Noller R B and Biondi A M, *Guide to Creative Action*, Charles Scribners' Sons, 1977.
Prince G M, *The Practice of Creativity*, Harper and Row, 1970.
Rawlinson J G, *Creative Thinking and Brainstorming*, Gower, 1981.
Rickards T, *Problem Solving Through Creative Analysis*, Gower, 1974.
Stein M, *Stimulating Creativity*, Academic Press, 1974.

BOOKS WHICH INCLUDE A SECTION ON IDEA GENERATION TECHNIQUES

Andrews B, *Creative Product Development*, Longman, 1975.
Crawford C M, *New Products Management*, Irwin, 1983.
Davidson J H, *Offensive Marketing*, Cassell, 1972.
Douglas G, Kemp P and Cook J, *Systematic New Product Development*, Gower, 2nd Ed, 1983.
Eastlack J O Jnr (ed), *New Product Development*, American Marketing Association, 1968.
Foxall G R, *Corporate Innovation*, Croom Helm, 1984.
Gerlach J T and Wainwright C A, *Successful Management of New Products*, Hastings House, 1968.

Hake B, *New Product Strategy*, Pitman, 1971.
Hilton P, *Handbook of New Product Development*, Prentice Hall, 1961.
Hisrich R D and Peters M P, *Marketing a New Product*, The Benjamin/ Cummings Publishing Co Ltd, 1978.
Holt K, *Product Innovation Management*, Butterworth, 1983.
King S, *Developing New Brands*, Pitman, 1973.
Kraushar P M, *New Products and Diversification*, Business Books, 1969.
Leduc R, *How to Launch a New Product*, Crosby Lockwood, 1966.
Marting E (ed), *New Products: New Profits*, American Management Association, 1964.
Morley J, *Launching a New Product*, Business Books, 1968.
Nash B, *Developing Marketable Products and their Packaging*, McGraw Hill, 1945.
Randall G, *Managing New Products*, British Institute of Management, 1980.
Scheung E E, *New Product Management*, The Dryden Press, 1974.
Urban G and Hauser D, *Design and Marketing of New Products*, Prentice Hall, 1980.
White R, *Consumer Product Development*, Longman, 1973.
Whitfield P R, *Creativity in Industry*, Penguin, 1975.

ARTICLES CONCERNED WITH ONE OR A NUMBER OF IDEA GENERATION TECHNIQUES

Barnett M K, 'Beyond market segmentation', *Harvard Business Review*, January-February 1968.
Baty G B, 'Generating a flow of new product ideas', *Machine Design*, 4 July 1963.
Carson J W, 'Three dimensional representation of company business and investigation activities', *R and D Management*, Vol 5, No 1, 1974.
Chisnall P M, 'Marketing research techniques for generating new consumer products', *Supplement to the Market Research Society Newsletter*, No 168, March 1980.
Clemens J, 'Synectics groups', *Advertising Management*, August 1967.
Clemens J and Thornton C, 'Evaluating non existent products', *Admap*, May 1968.
Fern E F, 'The use of Focus Groups for idea generation', *Journal of Marketing Research*, February 1982.
Fornell C and Menko R D, 'Problem analysis: a consumer based methodology for the discovery of new product ideas', *European Journal of Marketing*, Vol 15, No 5, 1981.
Frost W and Braine R, 'The application of the repertory grid technique to problems in market research', *Commentary*, July 1967.
Geschka H, Schaude G R and Schlicksupp H, 'Modern techniques for

solving problems', *Chemical Engineering*, 6 August 1973.

Geschka H, 'Idea generation methods in industry', *Creativity Network*, Vol 3, No 1, 1977.

Gordon W J J, 'Operational approach to creativity', *Harvard Business Review*, November-December 1956.

Greenhalgh C, 'Generating new product ideas', *Admap*, September, October, November 1971.

Greenhalgh C, 'Research for new product development', *Handbook of Consumer Research* (ed Worcester R), McGraw Hill, 1971.

King S H M, 'Identifying market opportunities', *Management Decision*, Vol 9, No 1, Spring 1971.

Kuehn A A and Day R L, 'Strategy of product quality', *Harvard Business Review*, November-December 1962.

Lanitis T, 'How to generate new product ideas', *Journal of Advertising Research*, Vol 10, Part 3, 1970.

MacDonald E A, 'Inventing new product ideas', *Esomar Seminar on new product research*, November 1970.

McPherson J H, 'The people, the problems, the problem solving methods', *Journal of Creative Behaviour*, Vol 2, No 2, 1968.

Morgan M and Purnell J, 'Isolating openings for new products in a multi-dimensional space', *Journal of the Market Research Society*, Vol 7, No 3, 1969.

Rickards T, 'Facing the need to innovate', *International Management*, April 1980.

Sampson P, 'Can consumers create new products', *Market Research Society Journal*, Vol 12, Part 1, January 1970.

Schlicksupp H, 'Idea generation for industrial firms — report on an international investigation', *R and D Management*, Vol 2, No 7, 1977.

Skelly F R and Nelson E H, 'Market segmentation and new product development', *Scientific Business*, Summer 1966.

Souder W E and Ziegler R W, 'A review of creativity and problem solving techniques', *Research Management*, Vol 20, No 4, 1977.

Tauber E M, 'Discovering opportunities with problem inventory analysis', *Journal of Marketing*, January 1975.

Von Hippel E, 'Users as Innovators', *Technology Review*, 1978.

Von Hippel E, 'Get new products from customers', *Harvard Business Review*, March-April 1982.

Waterworth D, 'Marketing: new product information', *Marketing Forum*, January-February 1973.

Wood J R, 'Conception and the birthplace of new product ideas', *Admap*, March 1967.

BIBLIOGRAPHY

Abernathy W J and Utterback J N, 'Patterns of industrial innovations', *Technology Review*, Vol 8, No 7, June-July 1978.

Achilladelis B, Jervis P and Robertson A, *Study of Success and Failure in Industrial Innovation*, Centre for the Study of Industrial Innovation, Sussex University, 1972.

Adams J L, *Conceptual Blockbusting: A Guide to Better Ideas*, Norton, 1979.

Andrews B, *Creative Product Development*, Longman, 1975.

Andrus R, 'Creativity: a function for computers or executives', *Journal of Marketing*, Vol 3, No 2, April 1968.

Angelus T L, 'Why do most new products fail', *Advertising Age*, 24 March 1969.

Bacot E (ed), *Marketfact*, No 48, 22 March 1979.

Baker M J, *Marketing New Industrial Products*, MacMillan, 1975.

Baker M J, 'Innovation – key to success', *The Quarterly Review of Marketing*, Vol 7, No 2, January 1982.

Barnett M K, 'Beyond market segmentation', *Harvard Business Review*, Jan-Feb 1968.

Barrett F, 'How to generate new ideas', *The Business Quarterly*, Summer 1975.

Barron F, *Creative Persons and Creative Process*, Holt, Rinehart and Winston, 1969.

Baty G B, 'Generating a flow of new product ideas', *Machine Design*, 4 July 1963.

Bessant J R, 'Influential factors in manufacturing innovation', *Research Policy*, Vol 2, Pt 2, 1982.

Blood P B, 'Britain's amateur marketers', *Marketing*, Jan 1979.

Booz, Allen and Hamilton, *The Management of New Products*, 1966.

Booz, Allen and Hamilton, *New Product Management for the 1980s*, 1982.

Bouchard T J, 'A comparison of two brainstorming procedures', *Journal of Applied Psychology*, Vol 56, 1972.

Bound J, 'New product research', *Supplement to the Market Research Society Newsletter*, No 168, March 1980.

Brown M and Rickards T, 'How to create creativity', *Management Today*, August 1982.

Brozen Y, 'Invention, innovation and imitation', *American Economic Review*, Vol 41, Pt 1, 1951.

Buggie F D, 'How to innovate', *Management Today*, September 1981.

Burns T and Stalker M, *The Management of Innovation*, Tavistock, 1961.

Cannon T, 'New product development', *European Journal of Marketing*, Vol 12, No 3, 1978.

Carson J W and Rickards T, *Industrial New Product Development*, Gower, 1979.

Carson J W, 'Three-dimensional representation of company business and investigational activities', *R and D Management*, Vol 5, No 1, 1974.

Child J, 'Organisational design and performance – contingency theory and beyond', *Organisation and Administrative Studies*, August 1977.

Chisnall P M, 'Marketing research techniques for generating new consumer products', *Supplement to the Market Research Society Newsletter*, No 168, March 1980.

Clemens J, 'Synectics groups', *Advertising Management*, August 1967.

Clemens J and Thornton C, 'Evaluating non-existent products', *Admap*, May 1968.

Cohen A B, 'New venture development at Du Pont', *Long Range Planning*, Vol 2, Part 4, 1970.

Cooper R G, 'The dimensions of industrial new product success and failure', *Journal of Marketing*, Vol 43, Summer 1979.

Crawford C M, *New Products Management*, Irwin, 1983.

Danzig F, 'New products', *Advertising Age*, 2 January 1967.

Davidson J H, *Offensive Marketing*, Cassell, 1972.

Davis E J, *Experimental Marketing*, Nelson, 1970.

Day R L, 'New products and market research', *Management Decision*, Autumn 1967.

de Bono E, *The Use of Lateral Thinking*, Jonathan Cape, 1967.

de Bono E, *Lateral Thinking for Management*, McGraw Hill, 1971.

Donnolly J H and Etzel M J, 'Degrees of product newness and early trial', *Journal of Marketing Research*, August 1973.

Douglas G, Kemp P and Cook J, *Systematic New Product Development*, Gower, 1983.

Drucker P, *Managing for Results*, Heinemann, 1964.

Duckley A, 'Planning the corporate zoo', *Accountancy*, July and August 1974.

Dunbar D S, 'New lamps for old', *The Grocer*, 3 April 1965.

Eastlack J O Jnr (ed), *Jew Product Development*, American Marketing Association, 1968.

Fern E F, 'The use of Focus Groups for idea generation', *Journal of Marketing Research*, Feb 1982.

Fornell C and Menko R D, 'Problem analysis: a consumer based methodology for the discovery of new product ideas', *European Journal of Marketing*, Vol 15, No 5, 1981.

Foster D W, *Planning for Products and Markets*, Longman, 1972.

Foxall G R, *Corporate Innovation*, Croom Helm, 1984.

Fraser J C, McG Beattie C, 'The impact of technological forecasting on marketing', *Technological Forecasting* (ed Wills G *et al*), Crosby Lockwood, 1969.

Frost W and Braine R, 'The application of the repertory grid technique to problems in market research', *Commentary*, July 1967.

Gerlach J T and Wainwright C A, *Successful Managment of New Products*, Hastings House, 1968.

Geschka H, Schaude G R and Schlicksupp H, 'Modern techniques for solving problems', *Chemical Engineering*, 6 August 1973.

Geschka H, 'Idea generation methods in industry', *Creativity Network*, Vol 3, No 1, 1977.

Gordon W J J, 'Operational approach to creativity', *Harvard Business Review*, Nov-Dec 1956.

Gordon W J J, *Synectics: the Development of Creative Capacity*, Harper and Row, 1961.

Gorle P and Long J, *Essentials of Product Planning*, McGraw Hill, 1973.

Grayson R A, 'If you want new products you'd better organise to get them', *Marketing in a Changing World, Proceedings of the American Marketing Association*, 1969.

Greenhalgh C, 'Generating new product ideas', *Admap*, Sept, Oct, Nov 1971.

Greenhalgh C, 'Research for new product development', *Handbook of Consumer Research* (ed Worcester R), McGraw Hill, 1971.

Gregory S A, 'The shape of ends and means: some aspects of morphological analysis', *Proceedings ASLIB Conference*, Oxford, 1974.

Hake B, *New Product Strategy*, Pitman, 1971.

Hamilton M, Sullivan V and Ward T, *Launching a New Product*, Institute of Marketing, 1970.

Harris J S, 'How to generate ideas for new products', *Business Management*, Vol 33, No 1, October 1967.

Hill P, 'Research and creativity in N P D', *Supplement to the Market Research Society Newsletter*, No 168, March 1980.

Hilton P, *Handbook for New Product Development*, Prentice Hall, 1961.

Hisrich R D and Peters M P, *Marketing a New Product*, The Benjamin/Cummings Publishing Co Inc, 1978.

Holt K, *Product Innovation Management*, Butterworths, 1983.

Jerman R E and Anderson R D, 'Marketing: a contingency approach', *The Quarterly Review of Marketing*, Autumn 1978.

Jewkes J, Sawers D and Stillerman R, *The Sources of Invention*, MacMillan, 1969.

Johne F A, *Industrial Product Innovation*, Croom Helm, 1985.

Kelner H W, 'Assessment of markets for new products', *Journal of International Marketing and Market Research*, Oct 1977.

King S, 'Identifying market opportunities', *Management Decision*, Vol 9, No 1, Spring 1971.

King S, *Developing New Brands*, Pitman, 1973.

Koestler A, *The Act of Creation*, Hutchinson, 1964.

Kraushar P M, *New Products and Diversification*, Business Books, 1969.

Kraushar P M, Paper presented to the Advertising Association Conference, reported in *Marketing Week*, 3 Nov 1981.

Kuehn A A and Day R L, 'Strategy of product quality', *Harvard Business Review*, Nov-Dec 1962.

Langdon R and Rothwell R (eds), *Design and Innovation*, Frances Pinter, 1985.

Lanitis T, 'How to generate new product ideas', *Journal of Advertising Research*, Vol 10, Pt 3, 1970.

Leduc R, *How to Launch a New Product*, Crosby Lockwood, 1966.

Levitt T, 'Marketing myopia', *Harvard Business Review*, July-August 1960.

Levitt T, *Innovation in Marketing*, McGraw Hill, 1962.

Lipstein B, 'Modelling and new product birth', *Journal of Advertising Research*, Vol 10, No 5, October 1970.

MacDonald E A, 'Inventing new product ideas', *Esomar seminar on new product research*, November 1970.

McPherson J H, 'The people, the problems, the problem-solving methods', *Journal of Creative Behaviour*, Vol 2, No 2, 1968.

Majaro S, 'The what and how of creativity', *Marketing*, Oct 1978.

Mandry G D, *New Product Development in the U.K. Grocery Trade*, Research Paper No 2, Retail Outlets Research Unit, Manchester Business School, 1973.

Marting E (ed), *New Products: New Profits*, American Management Association, 1964.

Marvin P, *Product Planning Simplified*, American Management Association, 1972.

Midgley D F, *Innovation and New Product Marketing*, Croom Helm, 1977.

Morgan N and Purnell J, 'Isolating openings for new products in a multi-dimensional space', *Journal of the Market Research Society*, Vol 7, No 3, 1969.

Morley J, *Launching a New Product*, Business Books, 1968.

Mowery D and Rosenberg N, 'The influence of market demand upon innovation', *Research Policy*, Vol 8, April 1979.

Mulloy J B, 'Research and the development of new products', *Admap*, August 1969.

Nash B, *Developing Marketable Products and their Packaging*, McGraw Hill, 1945.

Newell A, Shaw J C and Simon H A, 'The process of creative thinking', *Contemporary Approaches to Creative Thinking* (ed Gruber H E), Atherton Press, 1962.

Nielsen A C Co Ltd, 'The realities of new product marketing', *Nielsen Researcher*, Jan-Feb 1970.

Nielsen A C Inc, *How to Strengthen Your Product Plan*, 1966.

Nyström H, *Creativity and Innovation*, John Wiley and Sons, 1979.

Oakley M, *Managing Product Design*, Weidenfeld and Nicolson, 1984.

O'Meara J T Jnr, 'Selecting profitable products', *Harvard Business Review*, Jan-Feb 1961.

Osborn A, *Applied Imagination*, Charles Scribners' Sons, 1963.

Parker R C, *The Management of Innovation*, John Wiley and Sons, 1982.

Parker R C, *Guidelines for Product Innovation*, British Institute of Management, 1980.

Parnes S J, 'Effects of extended effort in creative problem solving', *Journal of Educational Psychology*, Vol 52, 1961.

Parnes S J, 'Education and creativity', *Teachers College Record*, Vol 64, 1963.

Parnes S J, Noller R B and Biondi A M, *Guide to Creative Action*, Charles Scribners' Sons, 1977.

Pessemier E A, *New Product Decisions: An Analytical Approach*, McGraw Hill, 1966.

Pessemier E A, *Product Management*, John Wiley and Sons, 1982.

Pilditch J, 'How to innovate', *Management Today*, August 1980.

Pollitt S, 'A practical approach to new products and new concepts', *Admap*, March 1970.

Prince G M, *The Practice of Creativity*, Harper and Row, 1976.

Quinn J B, 'Technological forecasting', *Harvard Business Review*, March-April 1967.

Randall G, *Managing New Products*, British Institute of Management, 1980.

Rawlinson J G, *Creative Thinking and Brainstorming*, Gower, 1981.

Rickards T, 'Facing the need to innovate', *International Management*, April 1980.

Rickards T, *Problem Solving Through Creative Analysis*, Gower Press, 1974.

Rickards T, *Stimulating Innovation*, Frances Pinter, 1985.

Rickards T and Carson J, 'Scimitar: a systematic approach to industrial new product development', *Paper presented at a seminar at Manchester Business School*, June 1980.

Roberts E D, 'What do we really know about managing R and D', *Research Management*, November 1978.

Rogers E M, *Diffusion of Innovations*, Collier MacMillan, 1962.

Rothman J, 'Choosing the best product ranges and assortments', *Management Decision*, Vol 5, No 2, Summer 1967.

Sampson P, 'Can consumers create new products', *Market Research Society Journal*, Vol 12, Part 1, January 1970.

Scheung E E, *New Product Management*, The Dryden Press, 1974.

Schlicksupp H, 'Idea generation for industrial firms – report on an international investigation', *R and D Management*, Vol 2, No 7, 1977.

Simmonds K, 'Removing the chains from product strategy', *Journal of Management*, Vol 5, No 1, February 1968.

Skelly F R and Nelson E H, 'Market segmentation and new product development', *Scientific Business*, Summer 1966.

Smith W, 'Product differentiation and market segmentation as alternative marketing strategies', *Journal of Marketing*, July 1956.

Souder W E and Ziegler R W, 'A review of creativity and problem solving techniques', *Research Management*, Vol 20, No 4, 1977.

Sowrey J T, 'The theory of imperfect marketing', *The Quarterly Review of Marketing*, Summer 1977.

Sowrey J T, *Idea Generation: The Sourcing of Ideas for New Products*, Doctoral thesis, University of Strathclyde, 1984.

Stein M, *Stimulating Creativity*, Academic Press, 1974.

Steiner G A, *The Creative Organisation*, The University of Chicago Press, 1965.

Stone M, *Product Planning*, MacMillan, 1976.

Tauber E M, 'HIT: Heuristic ideation technique', *Journal of Marketing*, January 1972.

Tauber E M, 'Discovering opportunities with problem inventory analysis', *Journal of Marketing*, January 1975.

Toll R, 'Analytical techniques for new product planning', *Long Range Planning*, March 1969.

Twedt N W, 'How to plan new products, improve old ones, and create better advertising', *Journal of Marketing*, Vol 33, No 1, January 1969.

Twiss B, *Managing Technological Innovation*, Longman, 1974.

Urban G and Hauser J, *Design and Marketing of New Products*, Prentice Hall, 1980.

Vernon P E (ed), *Creativity*, Penguin Books, 1970.

Von Hippel E, 'Users as innovators', *Technology Review*, 1978.

Von Hippel E, 'Get new products from customers', *Harvard Business Review*, March-April 1982.

Wasson C W, 'What is new about a new product', *Journal of Marketing*, Vol 25, July 1960.

Waterworth D, 'Marketing: new product information, *Marketing Forum*, Jan-Feb 1973.

White R, *Consumer Product Development*, Longman, 1973.

Whitfield P R, *Creativity in Industry*, Penguin Books, 1975.

Wills G, 'Technological forecasting. The art and its management', *Journal of the Market Research Society*, Vol 10, No 2, April 1968.

Wills G, Hayhurst R and Midgley D (eds), *Creating and Marketing New Products*, Crosby

Lockwood Staples, 1973.
Wood J R, 'Conception and the birthplace of new product ideas', *Admap*, March 1967.
Zwicky F, 'The morphological method of analysis and construction', *Studies and Essays (Courant Anniversary Volume)*, Wiley Interscience, 1948.

Index